30 EXERCISES FOR BETTER GOLF

Other Champion Press titles include:

- *Exercises for Better Golf (videotape)*
- *Women's Exercise Guide to Better Golf*
- *Play Ball! The Official Little League Fitness Guide*
- *Shoulder & Arm Exercises for Athletes*

Forthcoming Champion Press titles include fitness and conditioning programs for tennis players and skiers.

To order more copies of this book or Champion Press titles listed above, please call (213) 419-8669.

30 EXERCISES
FOR BETTER GOLF

FRANK W. JOBE, M.D.

MEDICAL DIRECTOR,
BIOMECHANICS LABORATORY
CENTINELA HOSPITAL MEDICAL CENTER

ORTHOPEDIC CONSULTANT, PGA TOUR

DIANE R. SCHWAB, M.S., R.P.T.

WITH

BILL BRUNS

Champion Press
Inglewood, California

Published by Champion Press
Centinela Hospital Medical Center
555 E. Hardy Street
Inglewood, CA 90307

Champion Press is a
registered trademark of
Centinela Hospital Medical Center

Manufactured in the United States of America

Library of Congress Cataloging-in-Publication Data

Jobe, Frank W.
30 exercises for better golf.

includes index.
1. Golf. 2. Exercise. I. Moynes, Diane Radovich.
II. Bruns, Bill. III. Title. IV. Title: Thirty exercises
for better golf.
GV979.E9J63 1986 796.352'3 85-73724
ISBN 0-936691-00-X

ACKNOWLEDGEMENTS

We've enjoyed writing this book, and want you to appreciate the information it contains. This kind of information doesn't just leap off a computer and into print without a great deal of effort by many people. Some of the most important contributors are mentioned in the text, but we'd like to cite them again, as well as take note of others who have been instrumental in bringing this project to fruition.

Russ Stromberg, President of Centinela Hospital, has been enthusiastic about the project and, indeed, first suggested putting this manuscript together. Ann McClanathan has provided organizational support throughout the project.

Daniel Antonelli, Ph.D., has been intimately involved with the analysis of the results. He also designed and built much of the instrumentation without which no data could have been collected.

Bitte Healy, M.S., R.P.T., and Brenda Larrivee, R.P.T., assisted in the important phase of research data collection.

Paul Callaway, R.P.T., shared valuable insights and clinical acumen about golf-specific injury patterns and injury prevention.

A number of exercises for strengthening and flexibility were adapted from the programs Clive Brewster, M.S., R.P.T. developed for patients at the Kerlan-Jobe Orthopaedic Clinic.

Alan Goldstein, of Centinela's Medical Photography Department, and Dennis Devine, Biomechanics Lab, provided essential photographic support. The illustrations so necessary for effective communication were drawn by Rik Olson.

Sol Shein and Michael Bass guided us through the treacherous waters of planning, design and production.

Jeanne Bertolli, of the Biomechanics Lab, lent her help whenever particularly knotty problems of language or procedure required expert input.

Special thanks must go to Lanier Johnson, and the group at Diversified Products, who provided much needed financial support and recruited many of the research subjects.

Art West, of the PGA TOUR, has encouraged the research project and been enthusiastic about its implementation.

Last, and perhaps most important, we'd like to acknowledge our gratitude to the professional golfers who allowed us to collect data and examine the particulars of their swing: Dave Derminio, Terry Forcum, Eddie Grant, Pat Lindsay, Tom Kite, Gary Koch, Hank Johnson, and Pete Kostis.

FWJ DRM

PREFACE

Every year, research of all kinds is conducted in laboratories around the world. Millions of dollars are spent, and many hours. Unfortunately, much of it never gets to the people who need it most. Not because it's not valuable. Just because it's not available to the public.

The information compiled to develop this book was gathered over a three-year period by studying professional golfers. The result is this simple program that any golfer can follow to reduce risk of injury, improve performance, and increase enjoyment of the game.

Champion Press is one of the ways Centinela Hospital Medical Center, a non-profit medical facility, demonstrates its dedication to improving the quality of life through excellence in medical care and active involvement in the community.

World-renowned for its accomplishments in biomechanics and sports medicine, CHMC is the natural source of information for athletes at all levels. As the official hospital for the PGA TOUR, the Los Angeles Lakers,

Dodgers, Kings, and Rams, and an official hospital for the 1984 Summer Olympics, Centinela is uniquely qualified and equipped for sports medicine research.

Future books from the Biomechanics Lab at CHMC include exercises designed especially for tennis players, swimmers, and women golfers.

CHMC also conducts research in many other fields. Ongoing studies in areas that range from chemical dependency to overall wellness will become the focus of future publications in this series.

Champion Press takes research from its ivory tower and puts it where it will do some good.

CONTENTS

INTRODUCTION

By Dr. Frank Jobe

People often ask, "Are golfers really athletes?" "Yes," I tell them, no question about it, for golf is a sport and to play it well, one must have athletic ability: strength, agility, coordination, and endurance. Unfortunately, the prototype golfer in the public's mind has long been the out-of-shape executive who rides a cart, plays 18 holes, and then retires to the 19th hole. Even at the professional level, golf has seldom been regarded as a sport that requires vigorous or specific body conditioning, especially when even pot-bellied players were winning major tournaments. The prevailing attitude was that walking 18 holes and spending time on the driving range was enough to keep the "golfing muscles" in shape.

These perceptions about golf are now changing, reflecting a growing awareness by amateurs and pros alike that a specific program of stretching and strengthening exercises will not only lower the risk of injury, but will improve performance—at every level of the game.

The exercises in this book were developed from

research projects investigating the movements of professional golfers during a swing. This research was conducted in the Biomechanics Laboratory of Centinela Hospital Medical Center in Inglewood, California. Our original intention was to design *sport-specific* injury prevention and rehabilitation programs for golfers. Yet as we evaluated our unique research findings, we realized we could translate this information into exercises that stretch and strengthen those muscles which play the most important roles in the golf swing. The result, we feel, is a well-focused exercise program that may help you perform at an optimal level plus decrease the risk of injury.

Although golf is not often considered a strenuous sport, its participants still sustain injuries connected with their play. We reviewed the medical records of the Kerlan-Jobe Orthopaedic Group in Inglewood for a recent 5-year period and found 412 patients with injuries attributed to golf. That's a considerable number of people for what is considered a "non-sport" sport. The most common injury was to the back, with the shoulder second, followed by elbow and knee injuries. (If *you* already have a golf-related injury, these exercises—under the supervision of your doctor—should hasten your rehabilitation efforts, because they are specifically related to the muscles you use in golf.)

It is not our goal in this book to provide an ultimate exercise program, but rather to describe and illustrate exercises for flexibility and muscle strengthening that are useful for golfers. Since muscle balance is important to athletic performance, these exercises should function as a sport-specific adjunct to a general conditioning regimen. Overall body conditioning (i.e., aerobic exercise) is the foundation on which all specific training programs are built. Such conditioning strengthens heart, lungs, and muscles and contributes to a healthy life, regardless of how often you play golf. Many such aerobic programs are available and you can select one which suits your personal needs and preferences, whether it be running, brisk walking, biking, rowing, aerobic dancing, swimming, or stationary biking.

Golf itself will not meet these aerobic demands, even if you're walking briskly from one shot to the next, since you must exercise at 70 percent of your maximum capacity for 20 minutes in order to give your cardiovascular system a meaningful workout. (You can calculate your maximum *working heart rate* by subtracting your age from 220. If you have had any cardiovascular problems, check with your physician.)

Still, you shouldn't underrate the benefits golf can provide—provided you walk. As my colleague, Dr. Robert Kerlan, has pointed out, "The golfer who rides a cart may be shooting a great game, but he is ruining a good walk in the process." When golfing, you're pursuing a whole-body exercise that enhances coordination and provides a certain tone to the muscles you use. This in turn should make a positive difference in how you feel about yourself.

The exercises in this book are the same ones now being used by a number of golfers on the PGA TOUR. Centinela Hospital is the official PGA TOUR hospital and we work with the DP Fitness Training Center (sponsored by Diversified Products) which travels from one tournament site to the next, providing a fully-equipped "gym" for the golfers. These pros have come to realize that golf demands more body conditioning than previously thought and, as a result, these exercises have become an integral part of their daily routine. The competition on the TOUR has become so keen and so deep, week after week, that they know they are not going to be in contention on the final day if they are not in top condition. Moreover, when they are in good shape and stretched out, they can work out longer on the driving range and know that they are not going to wake up the next day, and to the detriment of their golf game, feel stiff and sore.

There's not yet a large body of scientific research about the role of strength and conditioning in golf. Yet based on what our data will support, we're confident that the exercises in this book—done conscientiously—can help you play better. We're not golf coaches and we don't talk specifically about how to improve your swing, but your technique and scoring ability can improve in several ways. For example:

- By doing these exercises as prescribed and playing regularly, fatigue should not become a significant factor affecting your play. You will have greater muscle endurance and, therefore, be more consistent in striking the ball properly; and will more easily be able to recruit your muscles in the desired firing sequence throughout the round.

■ By swinging the way that you do now, but with greater strength in your golf-specific muscles, you will increase your chances of hitting the golf ball farther.

■ When your muscles are exercised in a golf-specific manner, you may eliminate certain swing faults. For example, as you acquire greater flexibility in the hips, this will lead to better body rotation as you swing, and thus better contact and more power at impact.

In short, this is our philosophy: Golf is a sport and you should try to approach it as a serious athlete. You will maximize your ability to hit the ball, while playing injury-free, when you are in good general condition and have exercised the muscles which are important to golf. But if you ignore the beneficial role of fitness, you must play with a self-imposed handicap. We want you to enjoy the game while playing up to your full potential.

30 EXERCISES FOR BETTER GOLF

CHAPTER ONE

Getting Started

Centinela Hospital Medical Center is widely known as a sports medicine center where professional and amateur athletes come for surgery, treatment, and rehabilitation. Centinela staff orthopaedists are the team physicians for Los Angeles professional teams in baseball, football, hockey, and basketball. They work with many teams and individual athletes in all sports throughout the country and in Canada.

In 1979, Centinela opened its Biomechanics Laboratory. It was designed to enhance Centinela's leadership in the sports medicine field, with sophisticated techniques and equipment for analyzing motion and developing improved procedures for rehabilitation and physical therapy. Since then, the Biomechanics Laboratory has conducted major research studies to learn more about how humans walk, climb stairs, run, stoop, reach, and perform at sports.

The pioneering research project with professional golfers detailed in this book is just one example of how state-of-the-art technology and advanced engineering are used to study body mechanics at Centinela. Sports medicine specialists in the Biomechanics Laboratory have also been conducting research into tennis, swimming, diving and baseball.

One notable success has been the Lab's research into the mechanics of the rotator cuff shoulder musculature, and how pitchers use and abuse it when throwing a baseball. Based on this research data, a series of stretching and strengthening exercises that help pitchers avoid a dreaded injury — a torn rotator cuff — was devised. (A booklet on this subject is being circulated internationally to professional and amateur teams, and a videotape is now available.)

The Lab also maintains computerized national records of professional baseball and football injuries (the Professional Baseball and Professional Football Injury Reporting Systems). These information systems, under the direction of Dr. Lewis Yocum, are tabulated to help prevent or reduce the frequency of similar injuries in the future.

While the professional athlete is often used as our research model, our ultimate goal is to have this data aid the average individual. For example, our sister corporation Centinela Hospital's Fitness Institute, is striving to improve athletic performances and prevent injuries through extensive research, equipment testing, training methods and educational programs. CHFI, founded in 1973, draws on medical experts from many specialties within the Centinela complex. These professionals help CHFI provide specialized health and fitness programs de-

signed to meet the individual needs of athletes, corporate executives and employees, and other citizens. These needs include fitness evaluations, executive fitness programs and overall health improvement.

In Dr. Kerlan's words: "There's a lot that can be done to help the vast army of recreational health oriented people. The Institute's main goal is to find out how healthy people work. Too often, people go for a checkup, find out nothing is wrong, and go away satisfied. They think they're healthy. But how healthy are they? We'd like to find ways to determine that, in a scientific manner, so we're continually gathering data."

While sports research is a high-visibility activity at the Biomechanics Lab, about half of its work involves applying its expertise and technology to solving other kinds of problems for people. For example:

- Many of Centinela's patients who have a joint replaced, such as a hip, have their gait analyzed before and after surgery. Length of stride, speed of stride, hip motion, and other factors are studied beforehand. The after-surgery examination can then determine how closely the patient is able to attain normal function.

- The Lab also examines the walking patterns of patients who have had a stroke, using a number of different braces, canes, or other walking aids. Analysis then determines which device or combination allows the most normal pattern. Similar gait analysis is done for children with cerebral palsy.

- By monitoring the movements of normal individuals, using the latest equipment to gather and computerize the data, the Laboratory enables the orthopaedic surgeon to devise preventive and rehabilitative programs for patients and to compare long-term effects of various surgical procedures.

Meanwhile, our golf-related research continues. In 1986, we will first assess the relative muscular contributions of the legs and arms to a pro's golf swing. Then we will test the forearm and upper arm muscles. As we conduct these studies, we will also try to settle some controversy about weight shifting during the golf swing,

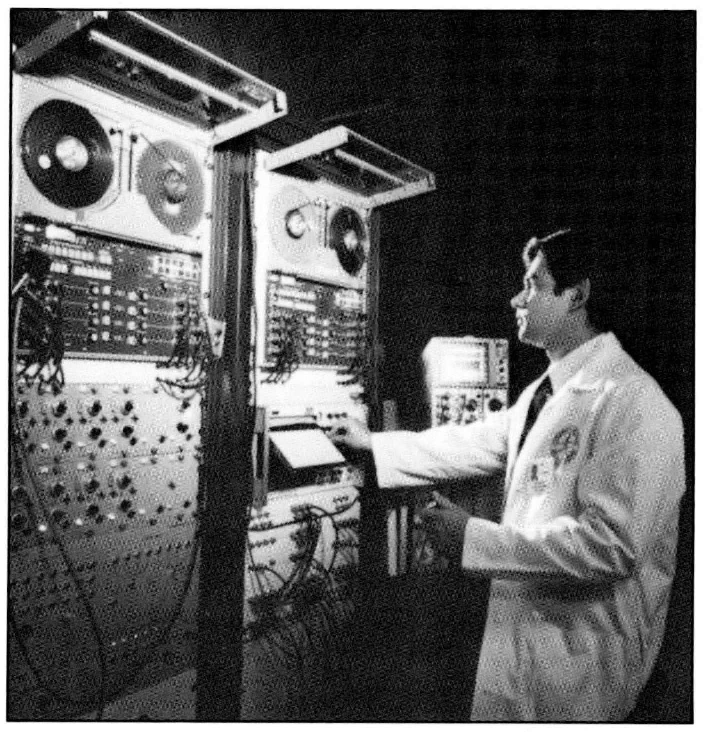

specifically, when the shift actually begins and the relative amounts going back and coming forward. Our research subjects stand on a force plate as they swing. This measures not only the downward pressure by the feet, but forward and backward forces.

Later, we want to investigate the muscular activity patterns of less flexible, less skilled amateur players at various handicap levels. These results will be studied separately and compared with those of the pros. Our hope is that we can then notice more ways to help the serious amateur golfer close the gap with professionals, at least in terms of strength and flexibility in golf-specific muscle groups—beyond what we've contributed in this book. This book, then, is but a beginning contribution to an exciting new field. We hope you find these exercises useful.

HOW THIS EXERCISE PROGRAM EVOLVED

Our investigation of the golf swing began in 1983, after we were approached by Dave Derminio, a long-drive champion from Walnut Creek, California. He knew about our Biomechanics Laboratory, and wondered if we had conducted any golf research. We told him we hadn't, and he volunteered to be a subject for whatever research we might do.

We investigated the research literature and found that, indeed, the golf swing had never been analyzed in a scientific manner to identify which muscles were being used as well as when, and how much they were being used. At this point, intrigued by the possibilities, we asked Daniel Antonelli, PhD, a biomedical engineer, to devise a research project that would assess this muscle activity and enable us to create a training program which would

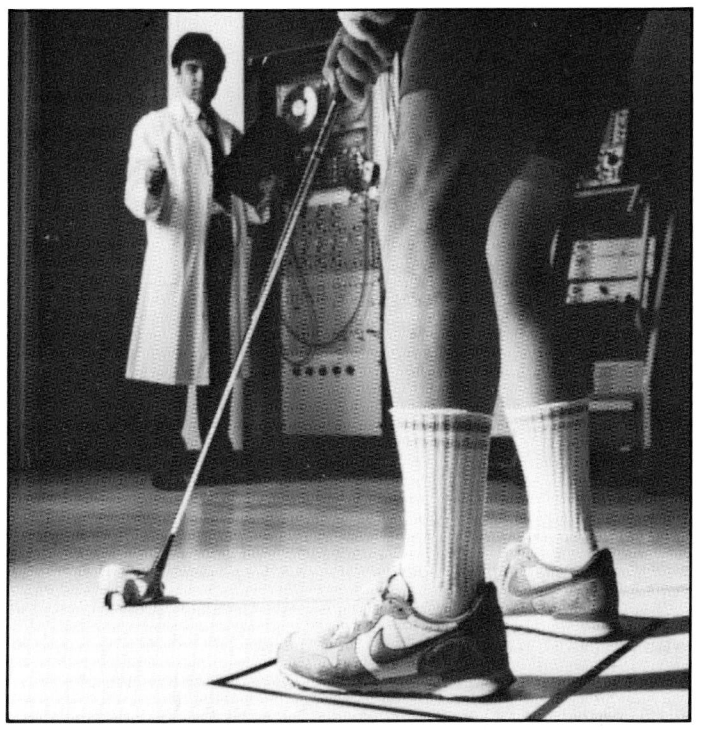

stretch and strengthen the appropriate muscles. At that point, Diversified Products, a major maker of fitness and recreation equipment, offered to fund much of the research. Independently, it had been investigating the mechanics of a golf swing in order to obtain quality information not only about golf but about fitness and conditioning as it related to golf.

This study was undertaken with the use of techniques Dr. Antonelli had developed to synchronize the muscle signals with high-speed photography, and was actually the first to investigate body mechanics in this way in order to find answers about muscle patterns during a golf swing.

HOW THE RESEARCH WAS CONDUCTED

The Centinela Hospital Biomechanics Lab evaluated eight male golfers, whose average age was 36: four touring pros (Tom Purtzer, Tom Kite, Gary Koch, and Pat Lindsey); two instructors (Peter Kostis and Hank Johnson); and two long-drivers (Dave Derminio and Terry Forcum). We tested the same eight players in each segment of the study—first the shoulders, then the hips—to provide an aggregate picture based on the same research subjects.

In order to monitor muscle activity, we relied on a modern procedure called electromyography. This procedure is based on the fact that whenever a muscle contracts, it gives off microvolts of electricity, and researchers can record this as a sign of activity.

Using 50-micron insulated wires (about the diameter of human hairs) as our electrodes, we inserted these wires into designated muscles with a hollow needle. These wires have tiny crimped ends which lodge in the muscle when the needle is withdrawn so that the wire remains inside.

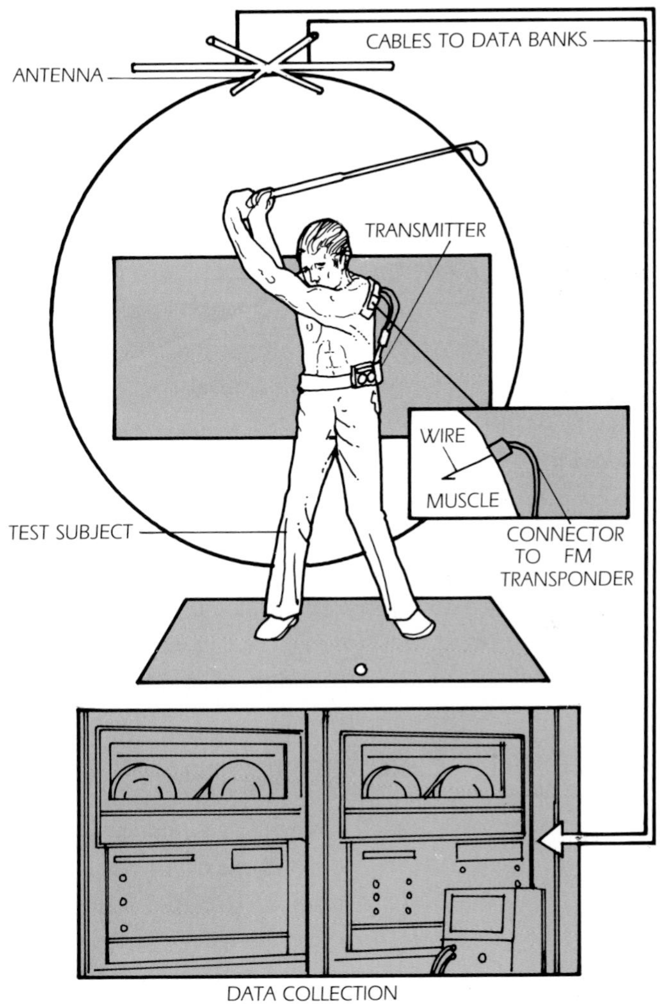
CABLES TO DATA BANKS
ANTENNA
TRANSMITTER
WIRE
MUSCLE
TEST SUBJECT
CONNECTOR
TO FM
TRANSPONDER
DATA COLLECTION

We monitored eight muscles individually in a designated area at one time. The wires from these muscles were attached to plates which were taped to the body and contained amplifiers. These plates were, in turn, attached to a transmitter with a battery pack worn on a belt at the waist. Each wire then acted as an antenna, recording the electrical activity as the individual muscles contracted. The signals from the wires were picked up by a main antenna and transmitted to a tape recorder. The tape was then read into a computer for interpretation.

Thanks to Dr. Antonelli's electronic telemetry system, we didn't have power cables interfering with the body as the subject took his full golf swing. Despite all this gadgetry, we tried to make the subjects as unencumbered as possible, and they said they were able to swing with out interference.

Prior to the actual testing, we had to determine the minimum and maximum activity boundaries for each muscle under scrutiny in order to draw accurate comparisons about the amount of muscular activity in each golfer. First we would ask the subject to relax as much as possible after the electrodes were inserted. This resting signal was fed into the computer and defined as zero activity for that particular muscle in that person. Then we asked for maximal effort from the muscles in which we had wires. This was set to equal 100 in the computer. (Physicians and physical therapists have a standard manual muscle test used for each muscle in the body when they are evaluating a particular problem. We used this standardized test, with each subject resisting in a certain direction and in a certain position, without swinging the club.) Thus, how hard the muscle actually worked during the swing could be placed within this zero to 100 range. Muscle effort was determined for every two milliseconds.

Once we were ready for testing, each subject was allowed to warm up until he felt comfortable. He was then asked to swing as he would normally, hitting a plastic ball. Activity was recorded by three 16 mm cameras set

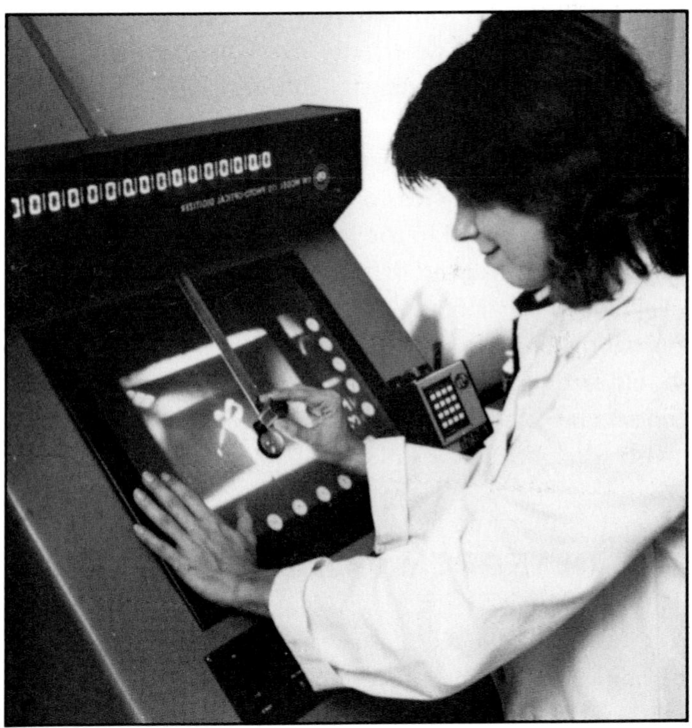

up around the lab, each one filming at 450 frames per second, which was fast enough to keep the clubhead in focus as it came down through the ball and to allow researchers to study the action in precise detail. All three cameras—one mounted overhead, one to the side, and one in front or in back—simultaneously filmed the subject in three planes. By having a counter on the right side of the film, we were able to view the body and the swing at the same instant in time, frame by frame, from three different perspectives. Meanwhile, by synchronizing this filmed information with simultaneous marks on the paper recorder, we could determine what muscles were firing and at what relative intensity during each particular instant of the swing.

Each subject swung the club four times to test a particular set of muscles on the right side. The equipment was then transferred to the left side and the entire testing procedure was repeated.

Since we already had considerable experience evaluating baseball pitchers, our first study dealt with shoulder muscle activity—the deltoid, the rotator cuff, and several other shoulder-girdle muscles. Our next study involved eight muscles in each hip.

THE RESEARCH FINDINGS

So what did we learn after all the many hours of testing, followed by the evaluation of the film and the EMG data?

1. A good golf swing has bilateral activity.

By studying both the right and left sides during the swing, we found that the golf swing is a balanced activity; the timing and the sequencing alternate, but the net muscular output shows as much activity on the left side as

on the right. This finding may not surprise you but remember: many instructors and golfers emphasize the left side, arguing that it provides the power for a right-handed golfer. Our studies of the shoulders and hips showed that the right side is at least as active as the left, and sometimes more so. The exercises in this book reflect our research by giving equal emphasis to both sides of the body.

2. The hips initiate movement into the ball.

One of the questions we wanted to answer was, "Do the hips push you through the swing or do they pull you through?" This has to do with the timing of the swing on both sides, and it's pretty clear from the data that hip muscle activity is initiated before the upper body turns into the shot—in other words, the hips pull you through.

3. Trunk rotation and flexibility are crucially important.

So far, the most noticeable difference we see on film when comparing professionals and amateurs is in trunk rotation (especially when the swing is viewed from above). We've noticed that older and less skilled players tend to get less than half the trunk rotation of a skilled and younger player. This lack of flexibility and strength is an important reason why people tend to play less well as they grow older, because they gradually lose the arc of motion which enables the body segments to transmit maximum velocity to the clubhead at impact.

Our stress on flexibility and trunk rotation isn't new, but this aspect of the golf swing hasn't received sufficient emphasis as far as determining how these affect where the ball goes and how consistently it goes there. Golfers give themselves a noticeable handicap by letting their available arc of motion diminish through lack of flexibility and by failing to realize the importance of body rotation. Why? Well, one way power in golf can be achieved is by rotating the body segments through space, and transferring energy from one segment to the next. If you diminish

the space through which these segments move, then you must use considerably more muscle power or effort to derive the same output. This means that to get the same clubhead speed at impact, you must "muscle" the club, and that puts added stress on your muscles. As the round progresses, these muscles can't do it all and they are prone to injury and hastened fatigue.

4. Rely on the large muscles of the body to generate power.

A closely related finding is that the large muscles in the body supply much of the power in a golf swing, and these muscles—especially in the hips (the abductors and extensors)—are quite active in a pro's swing. The hip muscles are the largest in the body and you must learn to use their potential power. Remember, a muscle's power is proportional to its cross-sectional area, meaning that the bigger it is, the more potential power it has. So you can see that no matter how strong your wrists and forearms might be, they cannot substitute for the proper use of your hip muscles.

Our research has given us a keen appreciation for the contribution made by the trunk and the lower body to what happens at impact. Thus we're encouraging all golfers to emphasize this part of the body instead of only forearms, wrists and hands. For example, we notice that less skilled golfers tend to swing the club primarily with their arms, while failing to use the power available to them in their trunk, hips and legs. The golfer who is a "hands-and-arms" swinger loses a tremendous amount of potential power by failing to get a good body turn that make use of the large muscles of the body.

In our research lab, the more we learn about the body's linkage system—the timing and sequencing of the body's segments as it performs an athletic movement such as the tennis serve or baseball pitch—the more we appreciate the importance of the hips. Basically, power in

golf comes sequentially, from the feet up as you rotate your body into the shot: energy is transferred starting from the legs through the hips to the upper trunk, then to the shoulders and out through the arms to the wrist and hands, and finally to the club itself. Understanding how energy is transferred through this chain of events is one thing; next you must master a swing that does the job for you, so that the clubhead speed at impact will produce the desired outcome. This challenge is outside the scope of this book, but we do know how important the hips are in that sequencing.

5. Skilled players are more efficient at using their muscles.

Skilled golfers are extremely efficient at using their muscles and their whole body when swinging the club, which is consistent with what the Biomechanics Lab has learned while investigating other sports such as tennis, baseball and swimming. When comparing the eight pros in this study with the amateurs tested to date, we've noted that the highly skilled players use a much lower percentage of their maximum muscular output potential as they swing.

6. The rotator cuff muscles in the shoulder play an important role.

Before we began investigating the golf swing, we knew from our research in baseball and tennis that the rotator cuff is much more important than previously thought in these activities. It was interesting to confirm for golf the similarly important role of the rotator cuff muscles on both sides of the body. In fact, the rotator cuff muscles in the shoulder need to be stretched and strengthened separately, with special exercises that are different from those done for the rest of the arm. This book contains the appropriate exercises for these muscles.

Typical shoulder exercises primarily work the deltoids, but we know from our research that this muscle, which lies along the top of the shoulder, is relatively "silent" during a golf swing, while the rotator cuff muscles are active.

THE ROTATOR CUFF FUNCTION

The rotator cuff is actually comprised of four muscles which underlie the deltoid muscle. Together, the rotator cuff muscles have an essential steadying effect on the head of the humerus, which is the long upper arm bone. The deltoid, the largest muscle of the shoulder, covers the shoulder joint and is used to raise the arm from the side.

We once thought that the rotator cuff worked only in synchrony with the deltoid during the golf swing; that

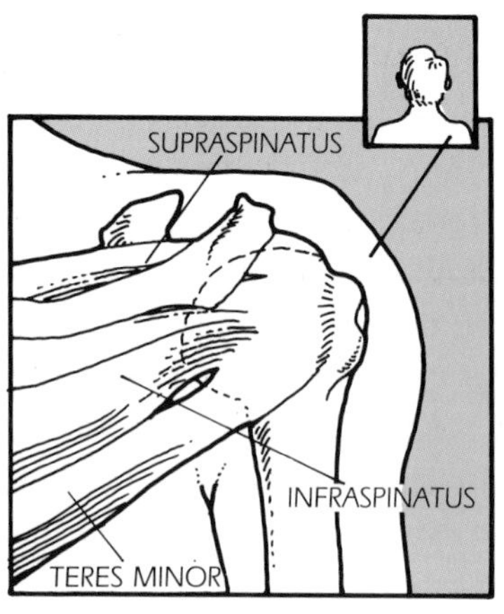

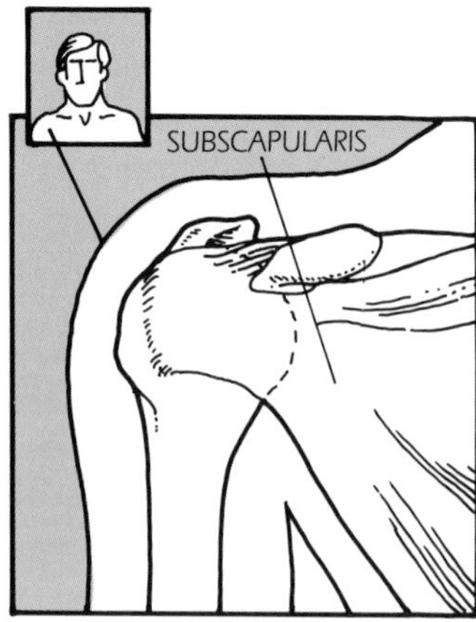

as the deltoid lifted up on either side, the rotator cuff pulled the head of the humerus down so that it slid under the shoulder blade. Yet our research showed that if you're swinging correctly, the deltoids contribute relatively little output on either side, while the rotator cuff does considerable work. In all the golfers we studied, the deltoid was virtually inactive throughout the swing.

The conclusion from our studies is that the rotator cuff muscles are responsible, in an almost isolated fashion, for turning the shoulder in and out and for swinging the arms out and back—on the backswing, during the acceleration into the ball, and on the follow-through. And since the rotator cuff functions independently of the deltoid, it must be strengthened deliberately to prevent superimposition of the more dominant deltoid.

PUTTING THE EXERCISES TO WORK

Once our research results were in hand, we began to design a golf-specific exercise program that would be effective for professionals as well as weekend players. Since our Biomechanics Lab is part of a health care community, our basic concern was to give golfers a conditioning program that would improve their strength and flexibility, thus lowering their risk of injury. Yet we also knew that when they exercised their golf-specific muscles on a regular basis, this would help them improve their performance by enabling them to play with greater consistency and endurance.

A number of golfers on the PGA TOUR began using the exercises described in this book, while also employing the exercise equipment in the Fitness Center sponsored by Diversified Products—a large tractor-trailer with expandable sides. Staffed by physical therapist, Paul Callaway, and an athletic trainer, Gene Lane, the van travels around the country from tournament to tournament, enabling the pros to receive personalized attention and making it convenient for them to maintain an effective fitness program throughout the golf season.

The pros who have been using these exercises tell us that just knowing they are in better shape gives them greater confidence so that they can play to their ability and practice hard. "If you can be stronger, more physically fit, you're better off," said Tom Purtzer, one of our research subjects. "Guys get tired late in the round, lose their concentration and their games slip. That happened to me, earlier in my career." Barry Jaeckel added, "Those of us who have been concentrating on the stretching exercises feel that we're not as sore after playing, we're not quite as injury-prone, and we have greater flexibility, which helps us swing the club the way we want to swing it. I feel that the stretching also helps me get more out of practice sessions. I'm practicing harder and more often now because I know if I work hard on the driving range after the round, I'm not going to suffer the consequences the next day."

Our hope, of course, is that you too will take advantage of the exercises in this book, by organizing them into a program that works best for you and your golf game. Keep in mind that these exercises are designed to help the widest possible group of golfers, regardless of age or ability levels. There are other ways to do some of the exercises and most could be done using sophisticated weight-training equipment. But our intent here is to get you into a golf-specific exercise routine with the least amount of stress and hassle, so that you actually put this book to use. These exercises allow you to start slowly, at your own pace, without any supervision, while still getting a well-balanced workout.

Ideally, for maximum benefit, you should do the flexibility exercises in this book every day, and the strengthening exercises three times a week, depending on your conditioning level and your golfing skill. If you're not in pretty good shape right now, it is a good idea to do your strengthening program on a day you don't play golf.

If you're wondering how soon you should start noticing the results and benefits of these exercises out on the course, we can't provide a set answer. Progress will depend upon your present conditioning level, your faithfulness in doing the exercises as prescribed, how hard you exercise, and your body's physiology, since we all develop strength and flexibility at different rates. In general, however, you should begin to recognize improvements in two or three weeks if you stick to your program. Consistency is all important. Your body will respond much better to a routine in which you do these exercises regularly—even if you must devise an abbreviated program—rather than doing all the exercises on a sporadic basis.

If you already belong to a health club, or have access

to exercise equipment, or if you have home exercise equipment such as the DP Gympac™ or other machines, then many of our exercises can be done on these machines. Simply show this book to a weight-training expert at the gym and tell him or her you want to work on these muscles and incorporate these exercises into a program. (Chapter 4 demonstrates how you might do these exercises on the DP Gympac™.)

One final suggestion is provided by the PGA TOUR therapist, Paul Callaway: At the end of every exercise session, try to find room to swing a club 10 or 12 times so that you use your body's improved flexibility and strength through the range of motion that you will use on the golf course.

IMPORTANT TIPS IN BODY MECHANICS FOR GOLF

It is interesting to note that most lower back injuries cannot be solely attributed to poor golf swing mechanics. The dilemma of back pain among golfers is compounded by years of improper body mechanics during teeing the ball, removing the ball from the cup, or prolonged putting practice. Common to all these three activities is that they involve bending forward at the waist. This forward bending dramatically increases the pressure within the intervertebral disks of the lower back. Consequently, frequent forward bending with your knees straight or bending forward while standing on one foot predisposes you to lower back injury while you play golf.

Therefore, to reduce the likelihood of lower back injury when you tee the ball and when you remove the ball from the cup, we recommend that you bend your knees while maintaining a straight or extended back posture. Furthermore, while practicing putting, you should take frequent breaks to stand erect and arch your back. This will help reduce chronic lumbar intervertebral disk pressure, and subsequent disk degeneration. For older golfers and individuals with knee problems, it is advisable to allow a caddie or playing partner to tee the ball and remove the ball from the cup. At the very least, when lowering yourself to a squat position and pulling back up to a standing position, use a golf club as a support. These tips, in combination with the exercises in this book, may keep you playing golf with fewer back problems for many years to come.

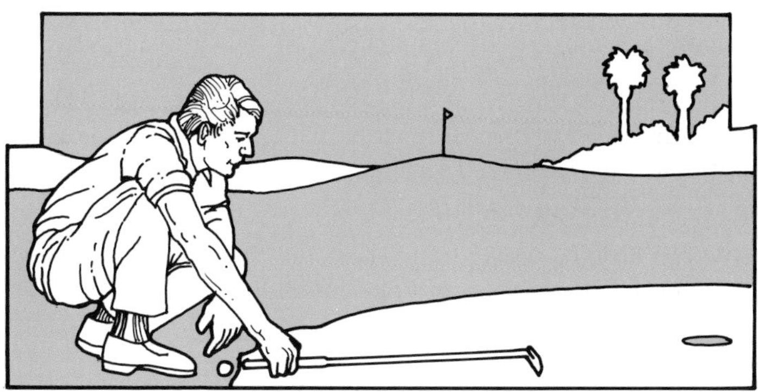

CHAPTER TWO

Stretching Exercises

While golf may not be considered a vigorous athletic pursuit by many of its players, the skill demands are high and require not only stroking ability but a conscientious conditioning program.

This chapter will focus on flexibility of the trunk and girdle musculature, which is necessary for playing golf well. The body's linkage system performs most efficiently when, through stretching, you allow it to work at its optimal length or tension. By elongating the tissues around the joints, you enable the joints to move through this greater range of motion. Muscles tend to shorten unless stretched on a regular basis. They work more efficiently, and with less risk of strain or injury, when slightly elongated.

Ideally, the stretching exercises presented in this chapter should be done every day so that you learn to do them from memory and they become a part of your daily routine. For optimal benefit, on the days that you play, these exercises should be done within 15 to 20 minutes of when you tee off. The value of stretching decreases when more than 20 minutes pass from the time you do your exercises until you actually begin to play.

FIRST, THE WARM-UP

Stretching exercises are best done after you've warmed up, so that you can stretch effectively and safely. A warm-up session literally warms up the body for a performance by elevating tissue temperature. One important effect of this elevation is that nervous impulses travel faster at higher temperatures, leading to more efficient performance. A slight rise in body temperature also promotes flexibility by loosening the connective tissues and improving the joint lubrication mechanisms. After warming up, the muscle fibers slide better, the joint lubrications work better, the gliding and sliding mechanisms are optimized, and you're much less likely to pull or strain a muscle. You can stretch without warming up, but not nearly as effectively or safely, so why make this effort to stretch for a less-than-optimal result?

An effective warmup will make you break into a sweat; until then, you haven't elevated your body temperature sufficiently. One way to warm up is to try running in place, or jogging slowly, or walking briskly, or even riding a stationary bike. Then once you are warmed up, begin your stretching exercises, for, as we mentioned before, the benefits of a warmup last only about 20 minutes.

If you tend to be a slow starter in golf, one important reason could be that you fail to warm up and stretch beforehand, thus forcing your body to perform with an extra handicap. Muscles that are warm and stretched out prior to teeing off are supple and loose, enabling your body to perform to its full capability. A proper warm-up session is also good prevention against minor injuries that can become nagging hindrances every time you play.

THE STRETCHES THEMSELVES

The following 10 stretches should help improve your flexibility, helping not only your golf game but your everyday activities. Here are several checkpoints to keep in mind:

■ During stretching, a muscle should be moved gently through the desired range of motion, so we recommend static as opposed to bounce-type stretches. During static flexibility exercises, a particular position is held for a period of time—normally 10 to 15 seconds. This requires greater effort and takes longer than a bouncing type of stretch, but you maintain the elongated position you seek. Static stretching also provides better feedback from the ligaments and tendons you are stretching; they warn you in time if you're going too far.

When you bounce as you stretch, you can usually go farther, but this poses a higher risk of injury because your body's momentum is harder to stop. Equally important, by not sustaining the stretch, you keep the tissues from elongating as effectively as they should. By concentrating on slow, steady stretching, the muscles must do the work rather than getting help from momentum.

■ Do each stretching exercise carefully, avoiding the tendency to rush or trying to reach too far at first. Move slowly and deliberately through your range of motion, and gradually try to widen it as your flexibility improves.

■ When you are learning, try to do these stretches in front of a mirror, so that you receive accurate visual feedback. Very often, a kinesthetic sense of how you are doing a particular exercise conveys incorrect information. When you can actually see yourself doing the stretch, you may realize that you're not doing the exercise the way it is pictured here in the book.

■ In general, when stretching, try to do about six repetitions on each side of the body so that you keep your muscles evenly balanced. Remember: golf is a bilateral game.

■ In the beginning, don't be discouraged if your body is tight and inflexible, and you have difficulty stretch-very far without discomfort. As you become more familiar with each stretching exercise and you become more flexible, you will find that it takes less time to attain the same amount of stretch. These exercises will become easier and you will be able to do them more quickly.

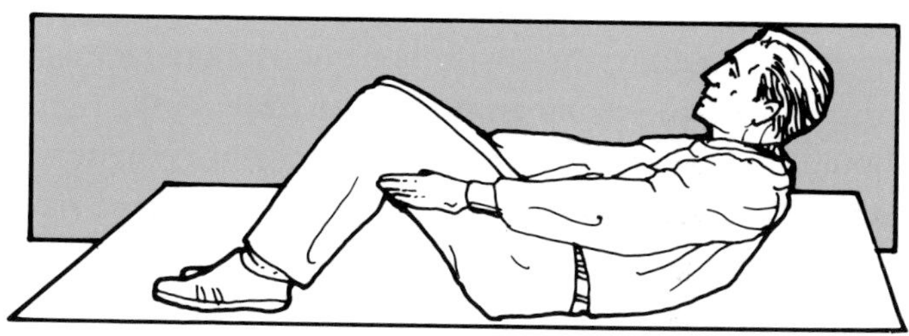

EXERCISE 1

Neck Stretch

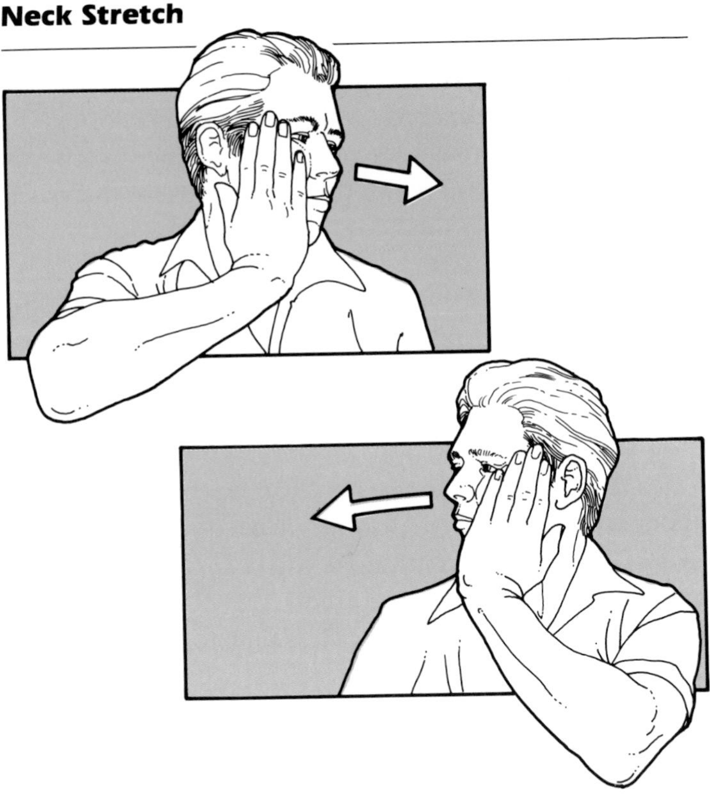

This exercise is an easy way to start your stretching sequence. Stand upright with your body facing straight forward, then look as far around as you can over the right shoulder—but don't cheat by turning your shoulders. Now take your left hand and push against the chin in that same direction. Hold for a count of 10 and repeat 5 times, then switch and look as far over the left shoulder as you

Neck Stretch (cont.)

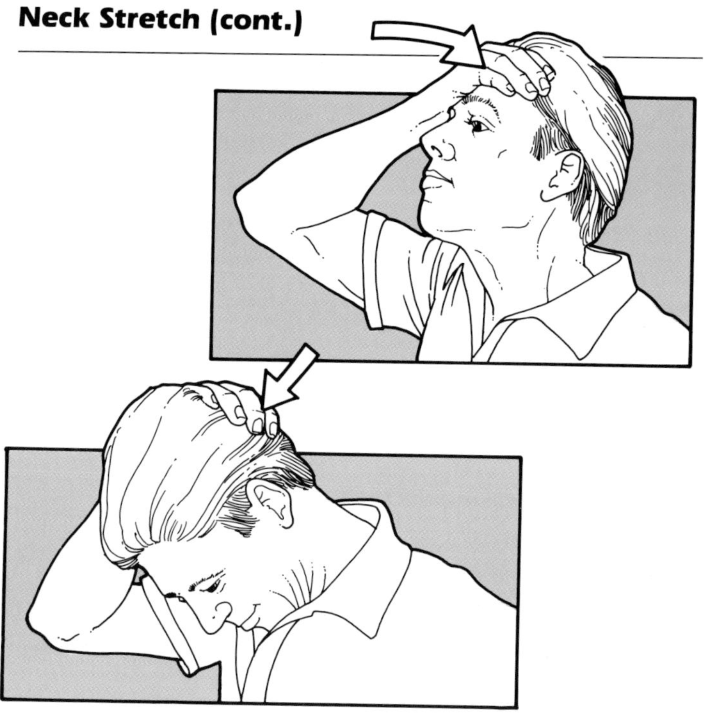

can. This time push your chin to the left side with your right hand. Hold and repeat.

Also do this exercise looking down, while pushing your head with your hand in the same direction, and then looking up, so that you're stretching the neck muscles in these directions as well. ■

EXERCISE 2

Rotator Cuff Stretch at 90 Degrees

The capsule around the shoulder joint needs to be stretched before maximum movement can be obtained. This stretch works the front of the rotator cuff, which comes into play on both sides of the body—first, as you bring the right arm back on the backswing, and then as

Rotator Cuff Stretch at 90 Degrees (cont.)

the left arm pulls through on the follow-through. You will feel the tension on this front side of the rotator cuff as you take your swing.

To begin this exercise, lie on a table with a small weight in your hand (two to five pounds). Start with your shoulder over the table edge and your elbow bent at 90 degrees, then allow the weight to pull your arm down gently in this position. Make certain that your shoulder is over the edge; otherwise you will be stretching your elbow.

Hold 10 to 15 seconds and repeat 5 to 6 times, then switch to the opposite arm. You should feel the stretch in the front of your shoulder. ■

EXERCISE 3

Posterior Cuff Stretch

Posterior Cuff Stretch (cont.)

This stretch increases flexibility in the back portion of your shoulder (the rotator cuff and joint capsule), which is involved on your left side during the backswing and on the right side as you accelerate into the ball and follow through.

Stretch the back portion of your shoulder joint by pulling your arm across your body, under your chin and as far back as you can manage, without rotating your torso. Hold 10 to 15 seconds, repeat 5 to 6 times, and then switch sides.

(The rotator cuff and posterior cuff stretches are a pair and ought to be included in your stretching routine for maximum benefit and to keep your muscle flexibility balanced.) ■

EXERCISE 4

Inferior Cuff Stretch

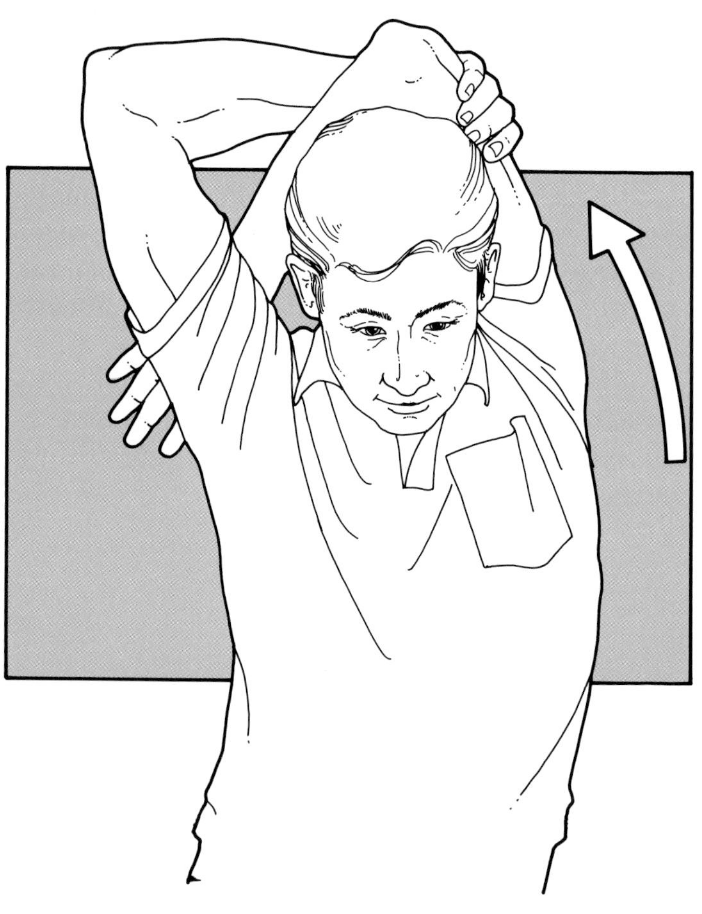

Inferior Cuff Stretch (cont.)

Thus far we have stretched the front and back of the shoulder. One part remains and that is the inferior or underneath portion. It is important to have as much potential to move in your shoulders as possible since your arms reach over your head during a good follow-through. These other portions of the rotator cuff can be stretched by reaching overhead and gently pulling on your elbow with the opposite hand. ■

EXERCISE 5

Chest Muscle Stretch

Golfers are often in a position in which their shoulders are rounded forward, and their hands are out in front, so that their chest muscles are tight and upper body movement is limited. The address position is a good example of this posture. This stretch will help you retain the maximum range of motion in this part of the body.

Using any corner, such as a room at home or where a row of lockers meets the wall at your club, put your forearms up against the adjoining surfaces and lean into the corner as far as you can. Be careful not to extend your neck, jutting the chin forward—just look straight ahead and let your body sink into the corner, so that you feel the stretch across the front of your shoulders. Push back to a starting position, or step forward to provide balance, and then start again.

Another way to do this is to pull both arms together behind you while standing or sitting very erect, with chin up and chest out. ■

Chest Muscle Stretch (cont.)

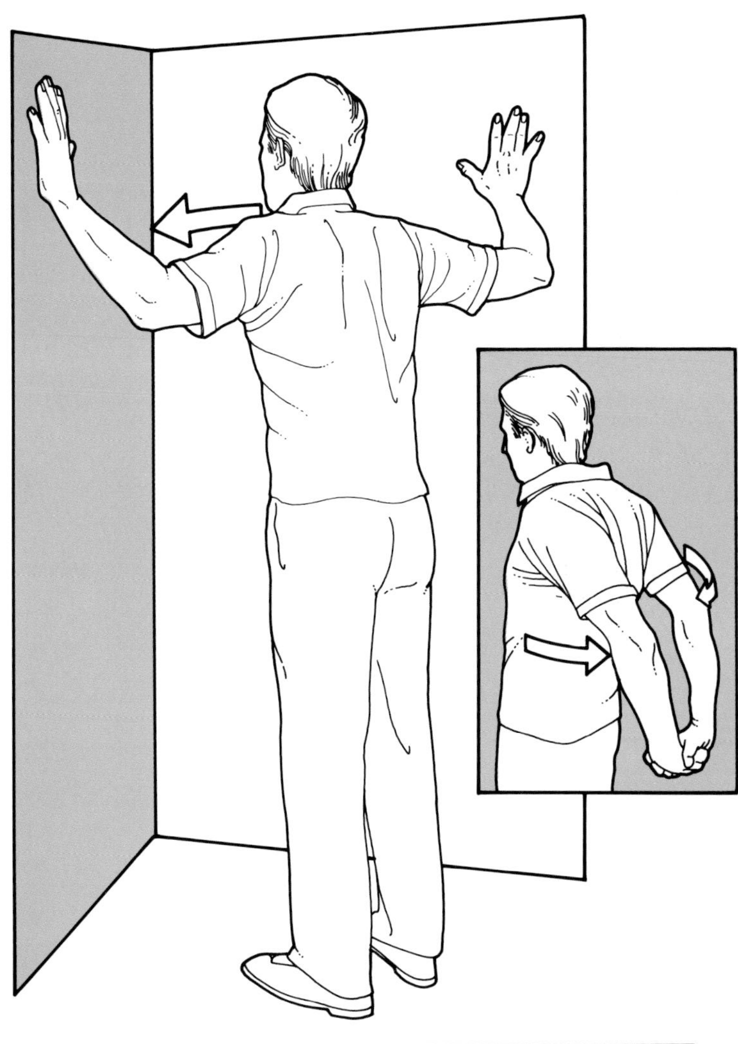

EXERCISE 6

Trunk Stretch

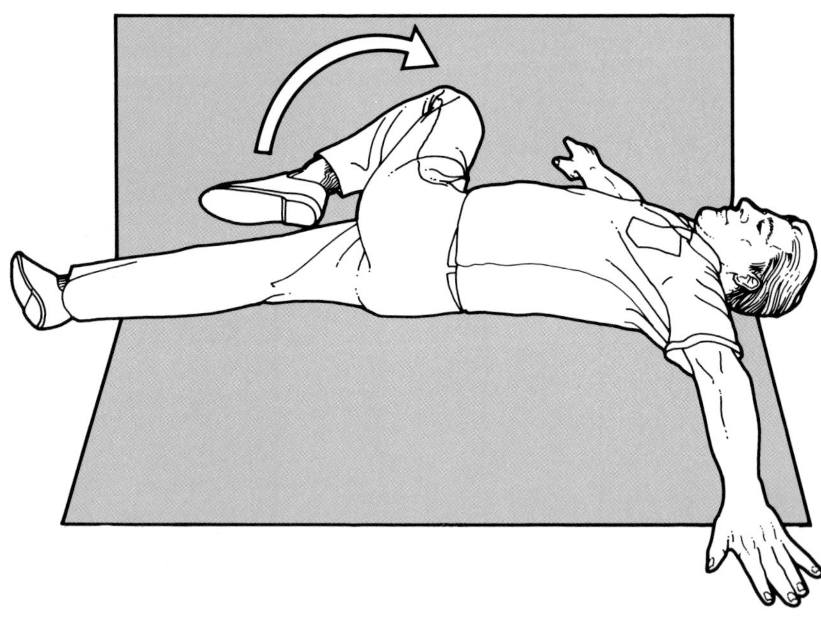

Trunk Stretch (cont.)

Trunk flexibility is extremely important in playing golf, for it allows the body to rotate properly during the swing. If you have a tight, inflexible back like most people, you are less able to rotate your spine through its potential range of motion. This particular exercise will give your back some of the stretching it needs.

Start by lying on the floor with your arms extended at shoulder height, straight out from the body. Now flip over on the side of your hip. Bend your left knee and cross that leg over your right, keeping your right leg extended and your shoulders *flat on the ground.* Now bring your left knee toward your chest and push it toward the floor. Hold for 10 to 15 seconds, then repeat. At first, try to do three or four repetitions on each side, and work up to about six times.

Make sure the torso does the work here by keeping your shoulders flat on the floor. The arms should keep you anchored—if your hands move, then you know the shoulders are moving. When you do this exercise correctly, you ought to feel a pulling sensation in the tightest part of your back. In general, the higher you bring the knee towards your chest, the higher up you will stretch the spine. ■

EXERCISE 7

Prone Press-up

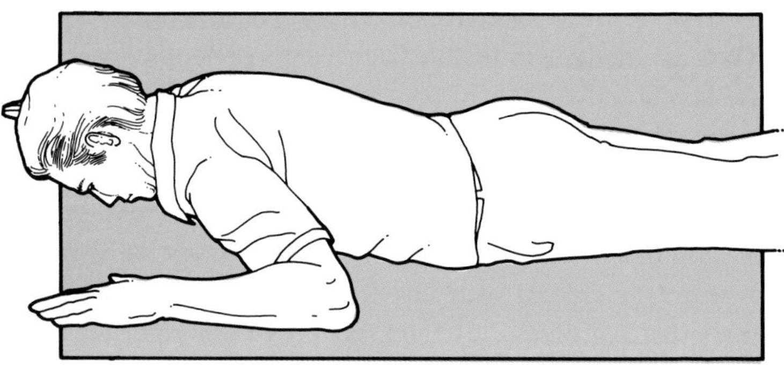

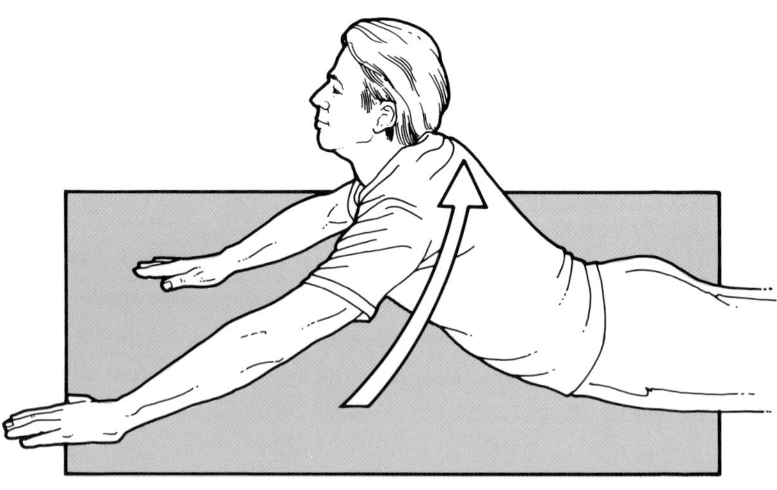

Prone Press-up (cont.)

Much of your daily living involves leaning and bending forward. Even on the golf course, every time you prepare to swing the club, your shoulders are rotated forward and your back is rounded. Since an over-emphasis on this posture can eventually lead to back problems, it's important to counter-balance that progression with back extension exercises.

Start this exercise by lying on your stomach and resting on your forearms. Now push up and back as far as you can manage, extending your arms but keeping your abdomen against the floor. Hold that position for a count of 10, then repeat.

You ought to feel this stretch at the waist and at your shoulder blades. To ensure this, make sure you keep your hips down as you lift your head back, so that you're pushing against the floor with your hands and thighs but letting your stomach relax and sink into the floor.

One precaution: if you have had a back problem, in the past or present, you should ask your doctor for advice. People with back pain often find this particular exercise uncomfortable to do. If you're in this situation, just start out very gently and use a modified approach. Instead of pushing up on your hands to extended arms, simply come up on your elbows and hold that posture. ■

EXERCISE 8

Single Knee To Chest

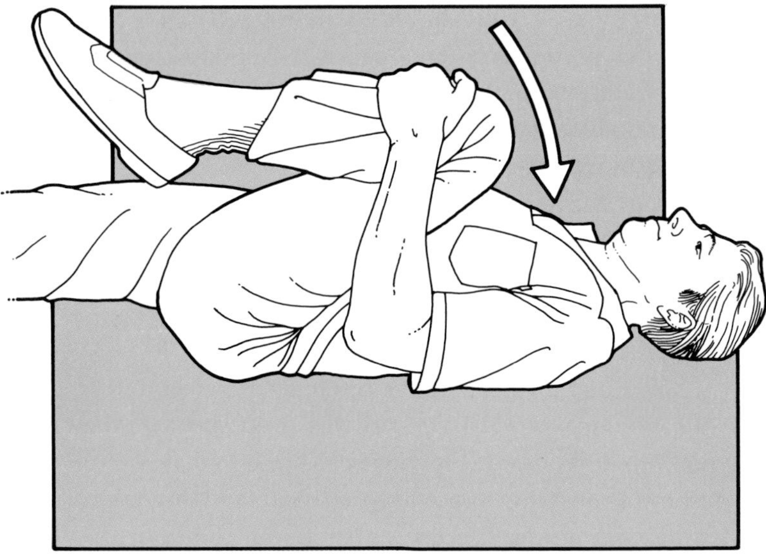

Most golfers have a tight lower back, which keeps them from using muscles in this area efficiently. The following two exercises will stretch the hip extensors, muscle groups which go across the lower back and hips and include the hamstrings and the gluteus maximus.

Single Knee To Chest (cont.)

Perform this first exercise while lying flat on the floor, on an exercise mat, or perhaps on a massage table. Straighten your right leg, then bring your left knee up as close as possible to your chest by pulling with your hands. Hold for a count of 10 and repeat 5 to 10 times, then switch sides. The non-involved leg must remain extended in order for this stretch to work. ■

EXERCISE 9

Both Knees To Chest

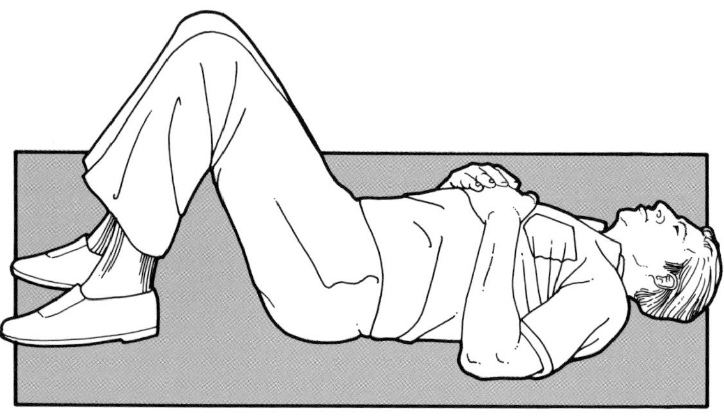

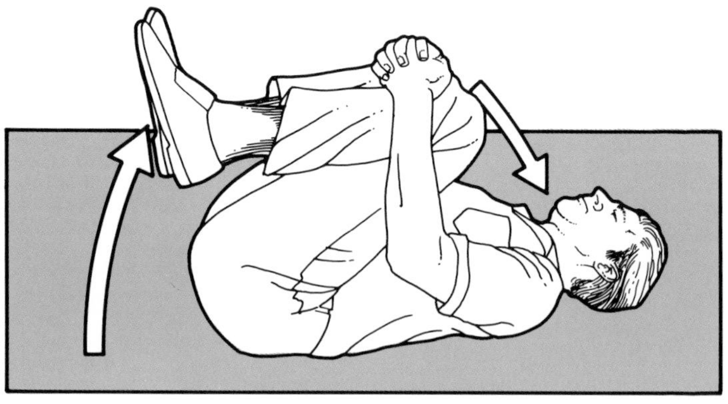

Both Knees To Chest (cont.)

Lying on your back, pull both knees up to your chest and hold them there for a count of 10. Relax and repeat five times. Performing this low back stretch with both legs continues the elongation process. If it seems as if you are spending a long time working on the low back, that is because it is one of the most serious problem areas. Without sufficient potential back motion, injuries occur more easily and you are forced to use your arms to "muscle" the ball through. ■

EXERCISE 10

Single Leg Stretch

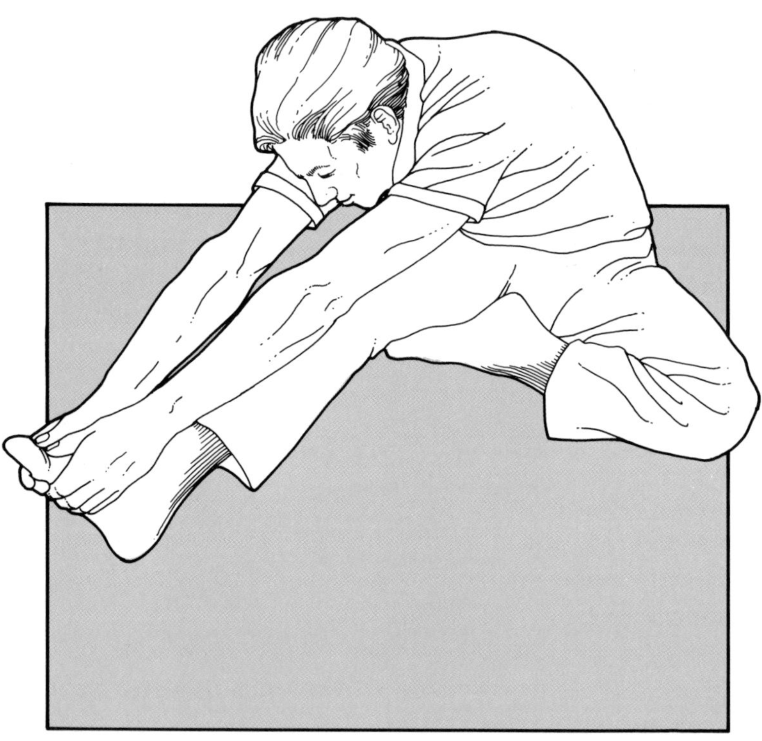

Single Leg Stretch (cont.)

This exercise should also stretch your hamstrings, the muscle group attached behind the thigh which flexes the knee and rotates the lower leg.

Start by sitting with your right leg extended and your toes pointed toward your head. Keeping your left knee as close to the floor as is comfortable, place the sole of your left foot against your right thigh. Then lean forward from the waist, keeping your right knee locked and reaching your hands out in front of you as far as possible. Try to reach your ankle or foot and bring your chin toward your right knee. Repeat five times, then switch sides.

In the beginning, very few people can actually grab their toes as illustrated here. If you can't reach this far, simply grab your knee and try to pull your chest down to your knees. Then as you progress, keep moving your hands down the calf, toward the toes. Eventually this will tell you just how much progress you are making and how much flexibility you are gaining.

You should feel this stretch behind the knee. If your trunk is typically rigid, you will also feel it behind your shoulders and in your back. Also look at your feet while you do this exercise, since this keeps your head up. If your head stays down, you may feel as though you are stretching properly when actually you're simply bending your neck. ■

EXERCISE 11

Side Bend

Side Bend (cont.)

Since a golf swing requires a combination of horizontal rotation and side bending, this exercise will help improve your lateral flexibility and reduce potential strain in your rib cage area

While standing, bring both hands over your head and lock your fingers with palms upward. Inhale, then exhale, and without bending forward, bend *slowly* to the side as far as possible. Return to the starting position, inhale, then exhale and bend to the opposite side. Repeat 5 to 10 times on each side.

Periodically check yourself in a mirror to make sure you're not cheating on this exercise. For example, in order to stretch the entire side of your trunk, you must bend at the waist and not simply drop the downside arm, which gives you the illusion of going further than you actually are. As you bend, strive to keep your elbows as straight as possible and the upper arm close to your ears. If you don't feel this stretch at the convex side of your waist, you're not doing it right. ■

EXERCISE 12

Lateral Hip Stretch

Although this exercise is seldom included in fitness books, it stretches the hip abductors effectively, which are the muscles that move your legs out to the side as you are rotating through the swing. Swing a club and you will feel the abductors at work on both sides.

Start by standing two feet away from a wall with your feet about shoulder width apart and your knees straight. Keeping your left foot flat on the floor, cross your right leg in front of the left as far as possible. Push against the wall with your right hand when you are standing straight, and bend to the right so that your whole body is in the shape of a 'c'. Hold 10 to 15 seconds and repeat 5 to 10 times. Since you're stretching one side and compressing the other, make sure you switch sides.

You should feel this stretch on the side of the hip corresponding to the arm which you have up against the wall. ■

Lateral Hip Stretch (cont.)

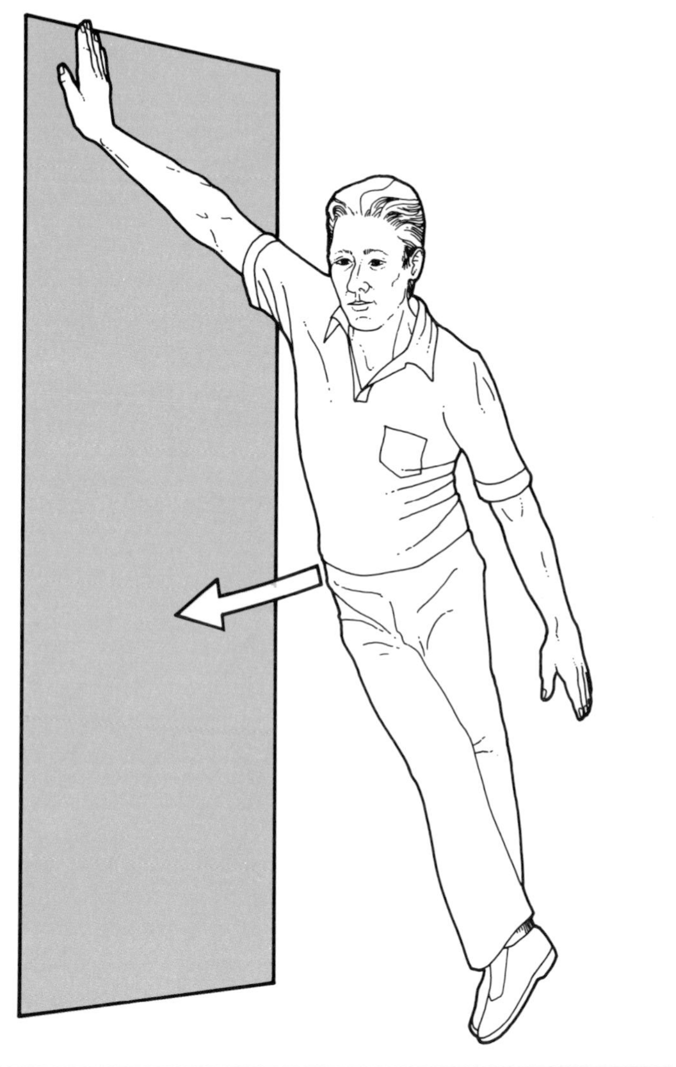

EXERCISE 13

Calf Stretch

Calf Stretch (cont.)

This exercise stretches the heel cords, and is an important preventive measure against Achilles tendon tears. Daily stretching of the heel cords is particularly important for women who wear high heels, since such footwear causes shortening of these tendons.

Stand upright about two feet from a wall, with your feet about shoulder width apart, then step back with one foot. Now place your hands against the wall at shoulder height and bend your front knee as much as possible, keeping your back knee straight and *both* heels flat on the floor. Hold and repeat, then reverse the positions of the legs.

You should feel this stretch in the back of your rear leg. If not, you may be lifting the back heel off the floor. Also, stand upright so that you get the stretching action where it's needed. This exercise ought to be done in bare feet, but if you do wear shoes, keep your legs further apart to compensate for the heel lifts. ■

CHAPTER THREE

Strengthening Exercises

Although it doesn't take enormous power to swing a golf club, doing so accurately and repeatedly requires strength and endurance. Traditionally, top golfers have relied on stroking technique and playing experience to lengthen their hitting distance. Weight training was for *other* sports, and not to be risked in golf, for fear that a muscle-bound body would prevent the golfer from swinging the club properly. Yet many pros now realize that they can benefit from a sport-specific strengthening program, either at home or in the gym.

The strengthening exercises here are designed to help you strike the golf ball with greater power and consistency, not to build rippling muscles, though they will give your body a firmer tone. If you can do these exercises three days a week, with a day of rest between workouts, you will find yourself playing better and hitting the ball farther with the basic stroking patterns you have now. If free time is a problem, you can shorten each workout by doing the arm and shoulder exercises one day, and the trunk and hip exercises the next.

These exercises can all be done using inexpensive hand-held or strap-on weights that are readily available at sporting goods stores. Use a minimal amount of weight when you start, since your goal is muscle toning and conditioning, not muscle bulk. In the beginning, body weight itself may provide enough resistance for some of the leg and trunk exercises. Most people start with two to five pounds and work up to about 10 or 15 pounds at maximum.

Initially, do each of these exercises slowly in a set of 10. Then as your strength increases, add a second and third set of 10 repetitions. Once you can complete three sets of 10 repetitions without undue difficulty, you may add additional weight. It is better to add more repetitions with the same weight as you grow stronger than to add weight.

If you're already in good shape, you may find that you can do two sets of 10 repetitions comfortably on each side for a particular strengthening exercise. But if you're sedentary, middle-aged and a non-exerciser except for golf, then one set of 10 repetitions may be all you can handle safely. Whatever your starting point, extreme soreness the next day indicates that you did too much and that you should back off. Keep doing three workouts a week, but lessen the intensity and gradually work your way up. Of course, if you have no muscle soreness the next day, then you should increase the demands of each exercise.

The exercises here should keep your golfing muscles well-balanced, provided you work both sides of the body during every workout. Remember, one reason we emphasize muscle balance is that the right side is at least as important to a good golf swing as the left side. Also, while our strengthening program is as golf-specific as possible, we're not trying to modify your anatomy so drastically that your golfing muscles become out of proportion to other parts of your body. These exercises work the front and back of the body, as well as the right and left sides, so as to avoid the long-range problems we've seen in other sports such as swimming and baseball pitching, in which unbalanced strengthening combined with relative overuse leads to injuries. In golf, if you overemphasize a particular muscle group, this can lead to various problems in coordination and execution by other muscle groups, not only as you swing a club but in other activities as well.

If you have access to weight-training equipment at your club or gym, you may want to show these exercises to the expert in charge and have him or her design an appropriate program for you to follow. However, our intent in this book is to motivate every reader to start doing these exercises at the easiest, most accessible entry level. (Some of these exercises, demonstrated using home exercise equipment from Diversified Products, are illustrated in Chapter 4.)

EXERCISE 14

Neck Strengthener

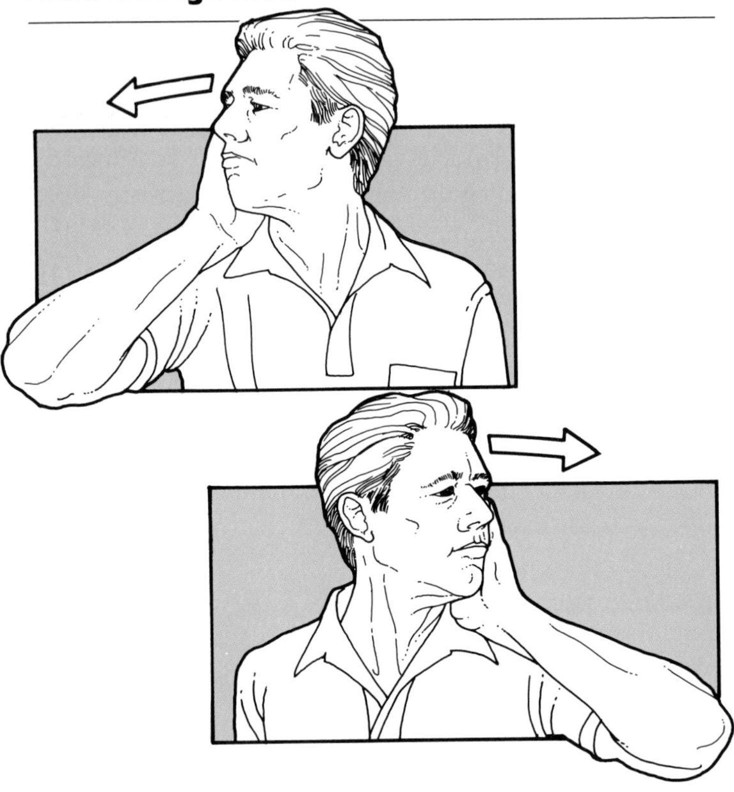

This exercise uses the same positions as those used to stretch the neck (Exercise 1, p. 26), only this time, as you look all the way over your right or left shoulder, try to push your face in the opposite direction, resisting that attempt with the opposite hand. In other words, if you are looking to the right, have your left hand push against

Neck Strengthener (cont.)

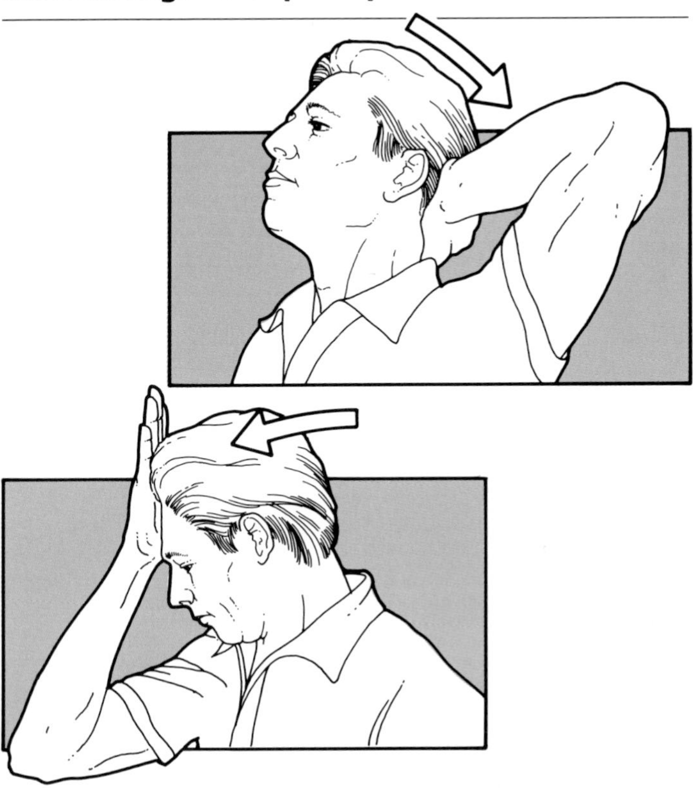

the left side of your face, as you try to turn your head back to the left.

You can also strengthen the neck by looking up or looking down, and then trying to move your head as you resist with the hand. Hold each time for 10 seconds and repeat. ■

EXERCISE 15

Rotator Cuff—Elevation

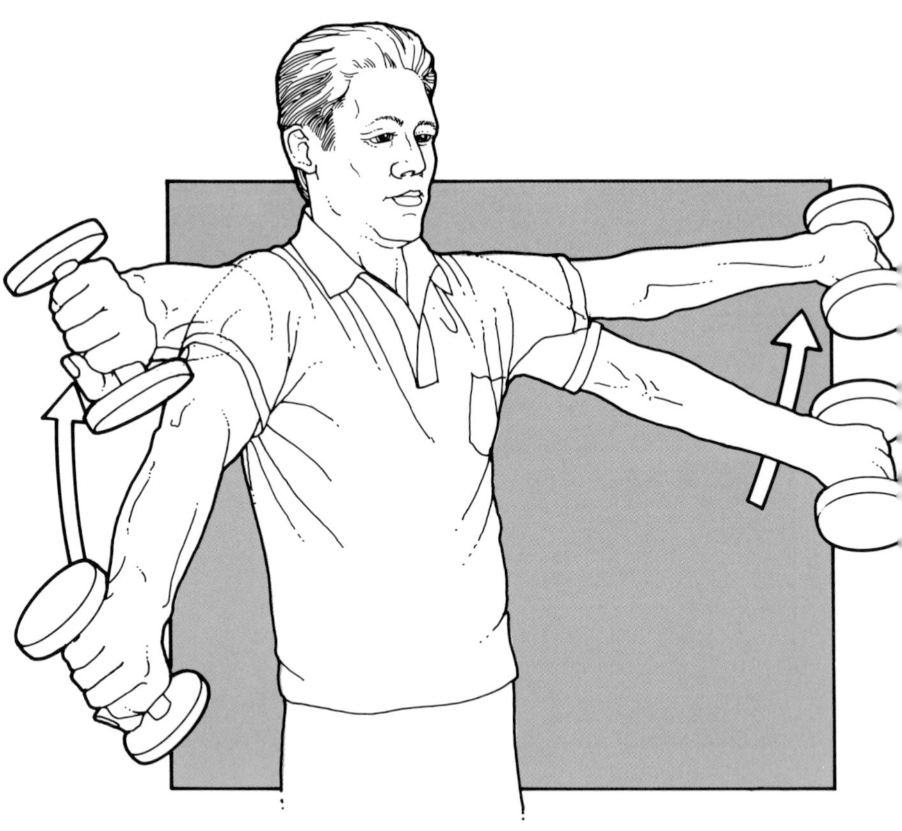

Rotator Cuff—Elevation (cont.)

The rotator cuff, as we noted earlier, needs to be strengthened separately from the other shoulder muscles. To do this exercise, hold light weights in your hands, straighten your elbows, and turn your thumbs toward the floor. Rather than extending your arms straight out to the side, slowly raise them in a plane about 30 degrees forward of that posture. Lift your arms no higher than just below shoulder level, keeping your body as still as possible, and then slowly lower them to the starting position and repeat.

If you already have a shoulder problem, lifting your arms higher than the shoulders can aggravate the injury. Besides, you can derive all the benefits from this exercise by simply going as high as we recommend. ■

EXERCISE 16

Rotator Cuff—External Rotation

This exercise will strengthen another part of the rotator cuff. Lie on your side with your head supported, and your elbow held close against your ribs and bent at 90 degrees. Slowly raise the weight until it is pointed at the ceiling, then lower it in a controlled fashion. Try to do up to 10 repetitions on this side, then switch. ■

EXERCISE 17

Rotator Cuff—Internal Rotation

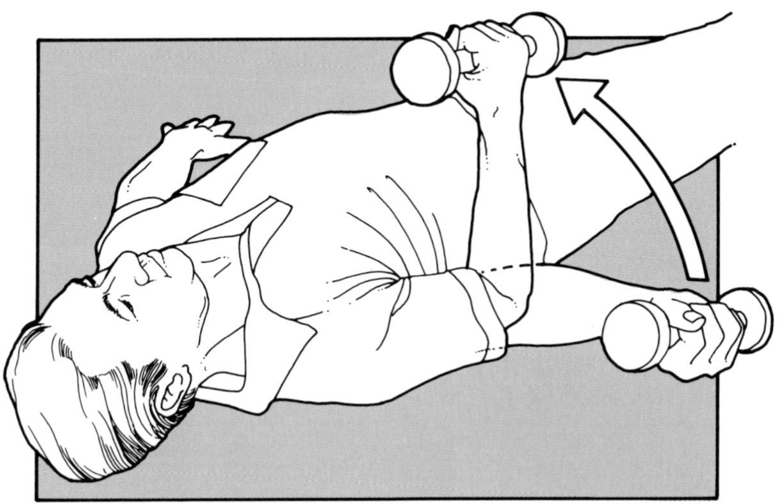

This third rotator cuff exercise is done as you lie on your back on a table or the floor. Again, with your right arm held close to your ribs and your elbow bent at 90 degrees, raise the weight until it is pointed toward the ceiling, then lower it back slowly to the starting point. This exercise strengthens the internal rotator part of the cuff. ■

EXERCISE 18

Shoulder Extension

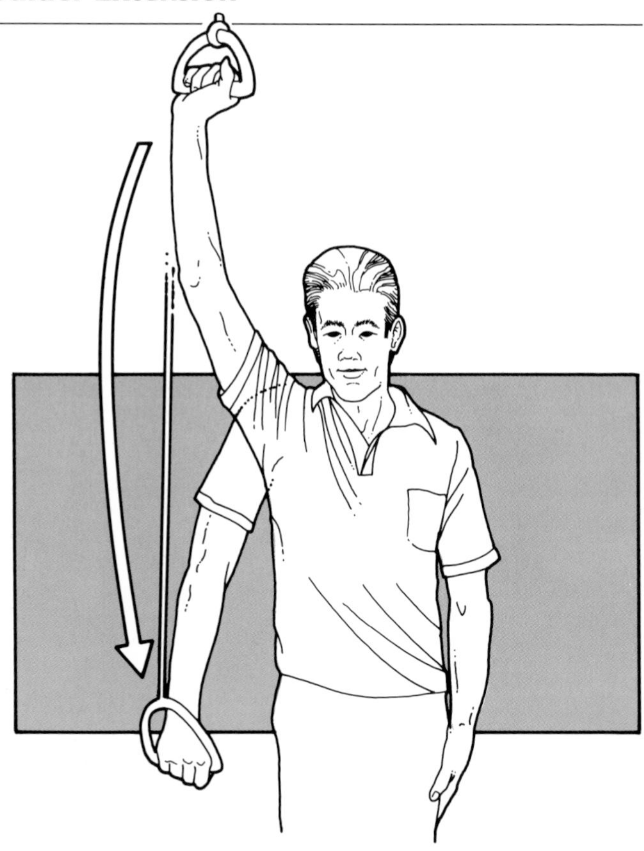

The *latissimus dorsi* muscle, which is located on your side, contributes power to the golf swing. An excellent way to exercise this muscle is to attach some elastic tubing overhead and pull down, so that your arm finishes

Shoulder Extension (cont.)

at your side. Try to work up to three sets of 10 repetitions on each side.

Surgical tubing or various types of rubber bands, such as Therabands™, are also available at well-supplied sporting goods stores. Whatever tubing you use should have enough elasticity to allow you to pull down comfortably 10 times. Try it out at the store.

An alternate way to exercise this muscle is to lie on a table and lift a weight up (as shown in the diagram). ■

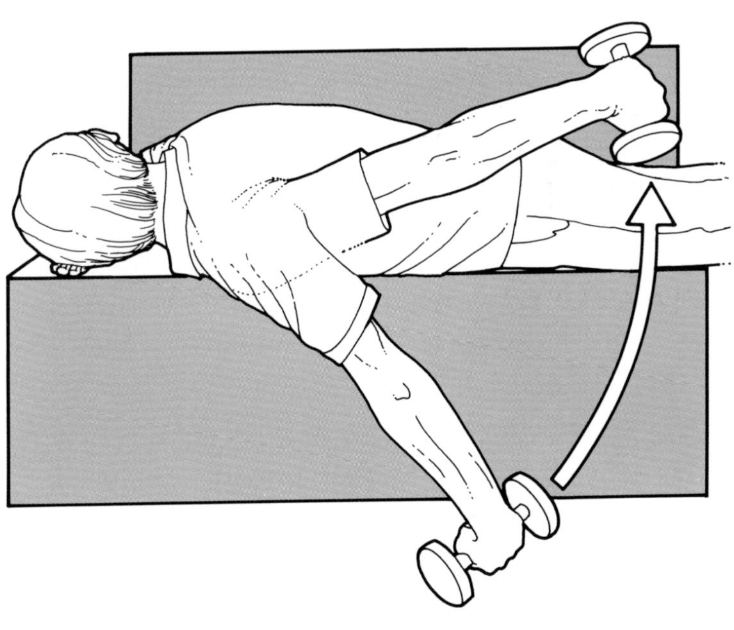

EXERCISE 19

Chest Muscles

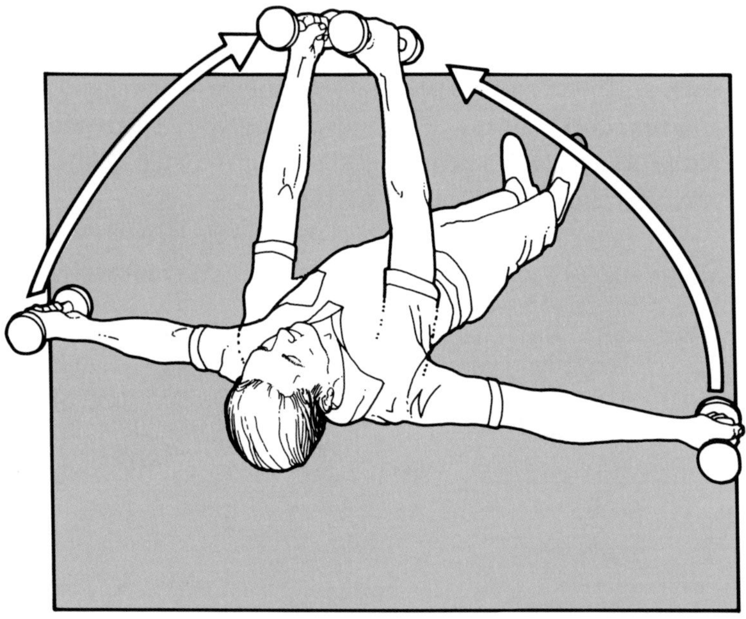

The *pectoralis major,* a large muscle of the chest, is important in carrying the arms forward as you swing—adding power on the right side and helping to control the descent on the left side during your drive into the ball.

Chest Muscles (cont.)

In this exercise, lie on your back, hold a weight in your hand, and extend your arm at shoulder level with the palm facing up. Then lift your arm until your hand is toward the ceiling, keeping your elbow straight. Lower your arm and repeat. Learn to do a set slowly, and then a set more quickly. This is done to imitate the speed of your arms during a swing. ■

EXERCISE 20 – 21

Wrist Flexion and Wrist Extension

The next six exercises should help strengthen your forearm muscles and your wrists. Strong forearms and wrists are important in golf, not so much to impart power, but to help you control the club properly during the swing. In a biomechanically sound golf swing, you want to transfer energy in a sequence—from your legs, to your trunk, to your shoulders and out to the club at impact. This energy is dissipated if the clubhead is wobbling. Since your clubhead is creating a long arc of motion, and is moving quickly through the impact area, the effects of a slight wobble, in terms of accuracy, are multiplied greatly.

Do this first exercise while you are seated, with your forearm supported on a table or on your leg, and your wrist over the edge, palm facing up. Lift the weight slowly, flexing the wrist, then lower the weight to the starting position. Repeat up to 10 times before switching sides.

Stay seated for this exercise, but now turn your palm down toward the floor. Keeping your forearm flat against the surface, lift the weight by extending your wrist up as far as you can, and then lower it to the original position. Remember to repeat with the opposite hand. ■

Wrist Flexion and Wrist Extension (cont.)

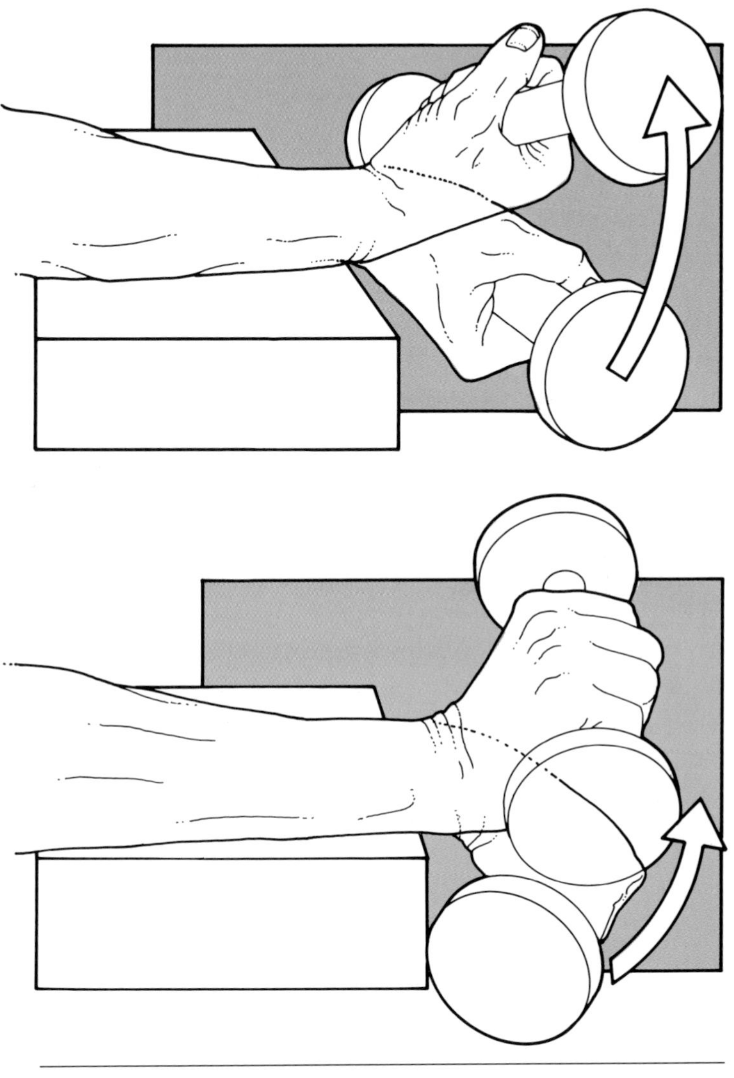

EXERCISE 22

Forearm Supination

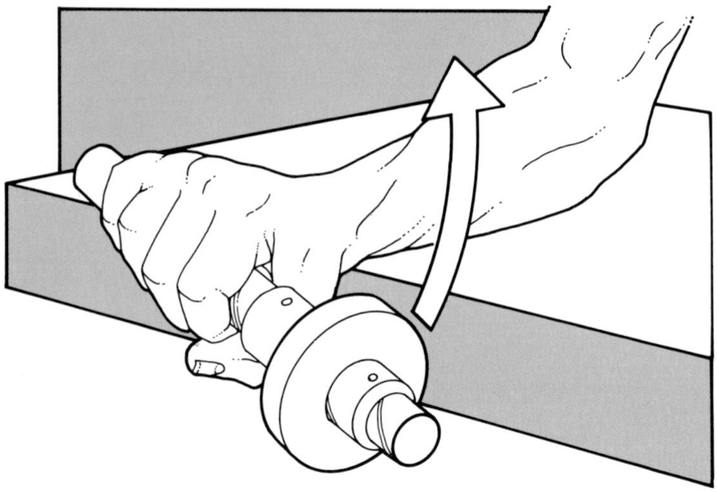

To strengthen the forearms, two separate exercises can be done. First, while seated at a table holding a bar weighted at one end, with your palm toward the floor, rotate your forearm until the bar is pointed at the ceiling.

EXERCISE 23

Forearm Pronation

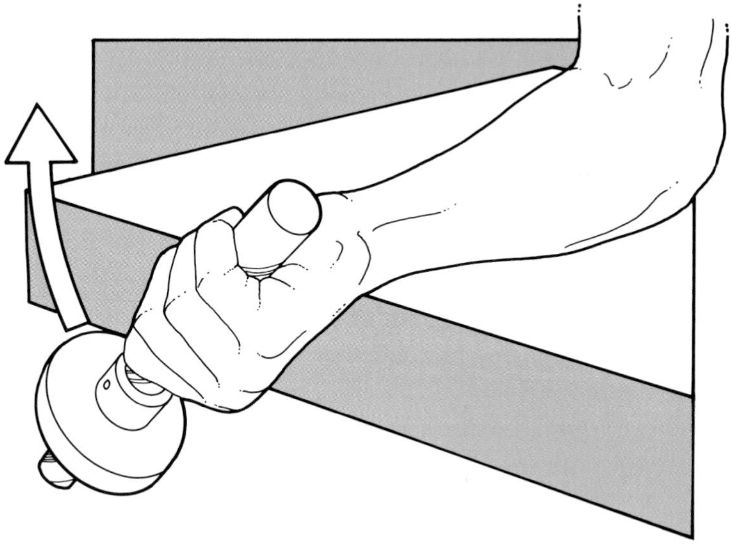

Remain seated, but this time keep the palm turned up while holding on to the weighted bar. Rotate the bar from right to left, until it is pointed straight up at the ceiling. Try to keep your elbow as motionless as possible. ■

EXERCISE 24 – 25

Wrist Bends

The following two exercises should strengthen the muscles which control the side-to-side motion which occurs at the wrist as you swing a golf club. These exercises should always be included with wrist flexion and wrist extension, so that you maintain relatively equal strength among the involved muscles, thereby gaining maximum benefit from strengthening the wrists along two separate planes.

Stand with your arm at the side, holding on to the end of a weighted bar. Lift the weight (as shown here) by bending your wrist laterally toward the small finger side of your hand. Return slowly to the starting position. Repeat with the opposite arm.

Assume the same position as in the previous exercise, but lift the weight laterally toward the thumb side of your hand. Return slowly to the starting position and repeat. Then work the opposite arm. ■

Wrist Bends (cont.)

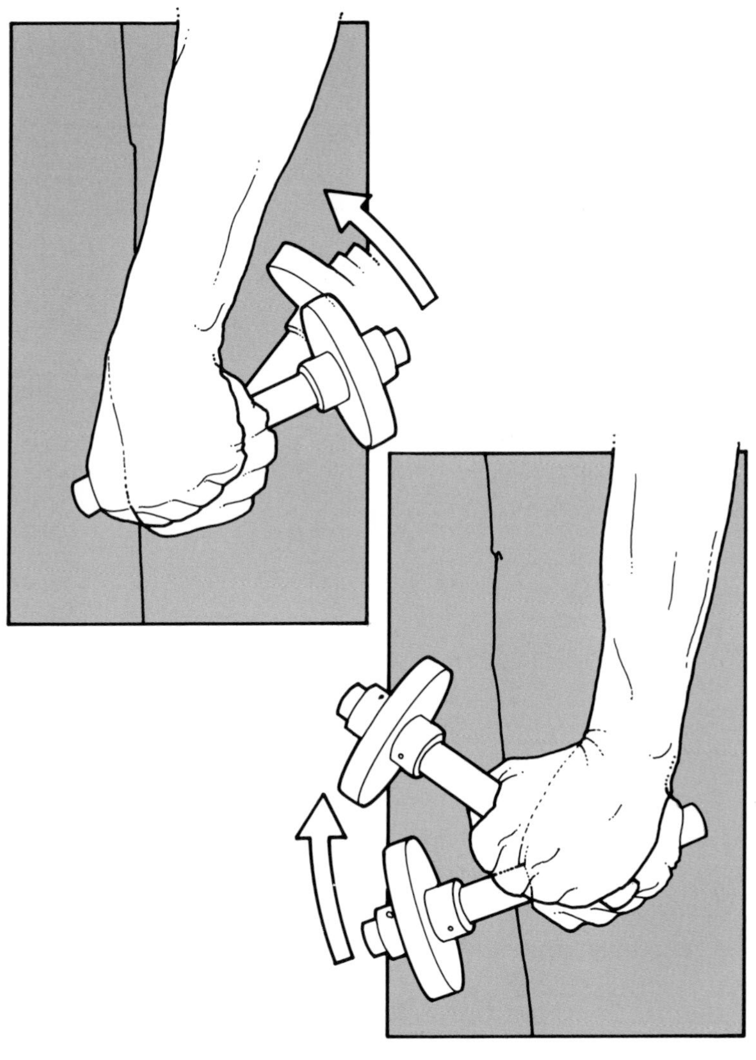

EXERCISE 26

Abdominal Curl

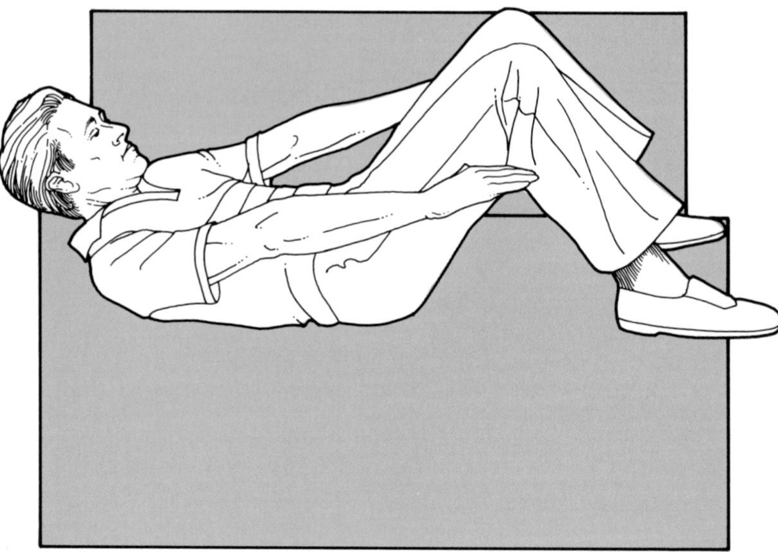

This exercise is the safest and most efficient way to strengthen the abdominal muscles.

Lie on your back with your knees bent approximately 90 degrees, and your feet flat on the ground. Neither your knees nor your toes should be hooked underneath anything, since this lessens the exercise's effectiveness

Abdominal Curl (cont.)

working the abdominals. Extend your arms toward your feet, with palms down. Now lift your torso only until your shoulders clear the floor. Hold for five seconds while exhaling, then lie back down.

Most people are unable to do this exercise more than 10 times at first. With practice, however, you will be able to repeat it 20 to 30 times. As you become stronger, cross your arms over your chest, instead of extending them. Next, try to put your hands behind your head, for this will result in even greater benefits for the same amount of exercise time.

At first, you may question how this exercise can be so effective, since you raise your torso such a short distance. But we know that simply clearing your shoulder blades from the floor and holding to a count of five gives your stomach muscles the maximum benefit. Moving all the way up, for a traditional situp, simply uses different muscles (the hip flexors) while adding more strain if you happen to have an existing back problem.

To strengthen your abdominals in a slightly different way, so that they can handle the twisting and turning that occurs during a good golf swing, we recommend doing this same exercise on the diagonal. Do this by leaning your left shoulder toward the right hip as you raise up, and then the right shoulder toward the left hip. ■

EXERCISE 27

Opposite Arm and Leg Lift

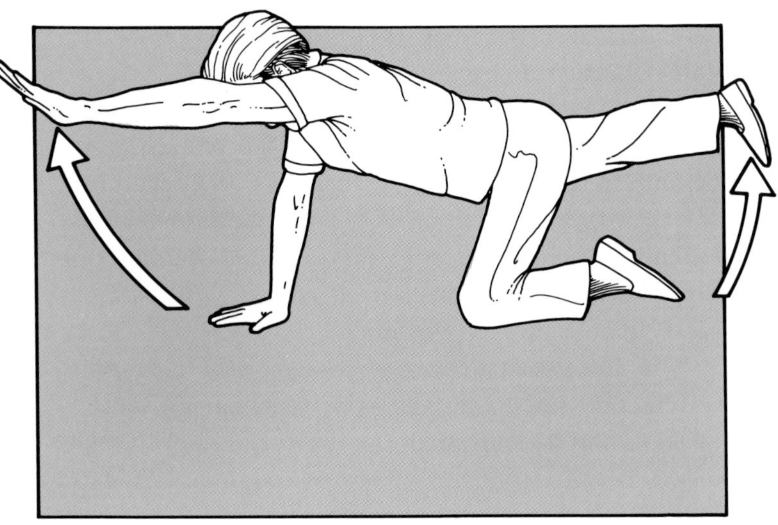

Here's an excellent exercise to strengthen the extensor muscles in your back. Starting out on your hands and knees, raise the left arm and the right leg and extend them straight out. Hold for a count of 10 (which is not easy) and then slowly lower them to the floor. Repeat with the

Opposite Arm and Leg Lift (cont.)

same arm and leg and try to 10 repetitions. Don't switch after every exercise; complete a set of 10 using the same arm and leg. Then you can switch to the opposite arm and leg (right arm and left leg) and start another set of 10. ■

EXERCISE 28

Side Leg Lift

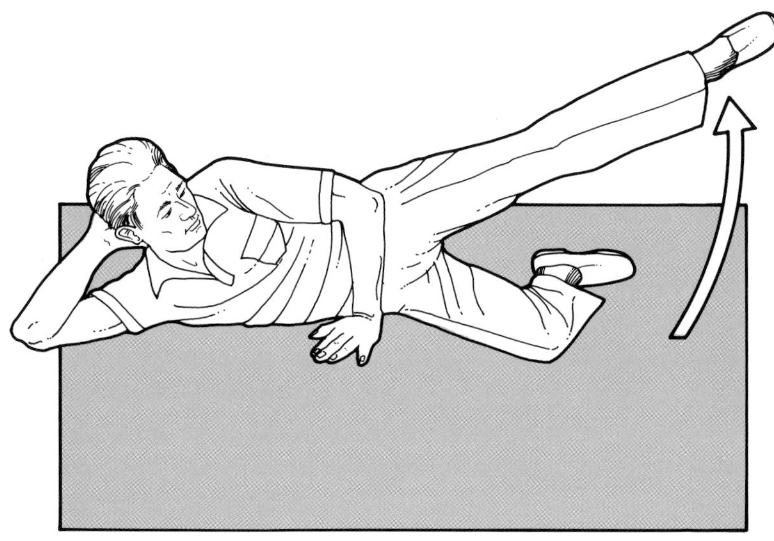

We've stressed the important role played by the hip muscles as you rotate in the golf swing and drive through the ball. This exercise works on the hip abductors.

Lie on the floor on your right side, with your head supported and your right leg flexed at the knee. Lift your left leg straight up as high as you can, with the knee held

Side Leg Lift (cont.)

straight. Hold this position for 3 to 5 seconds, then slowly return to the starting position. Try for 10 repetitions, then repeat on the opposite side.

In performing this exercise, make sure you do not rotate your hips or allow them to bend forward, since this forces you to compensate with other muscles. ■

EXERCISE 29

Hip Extension

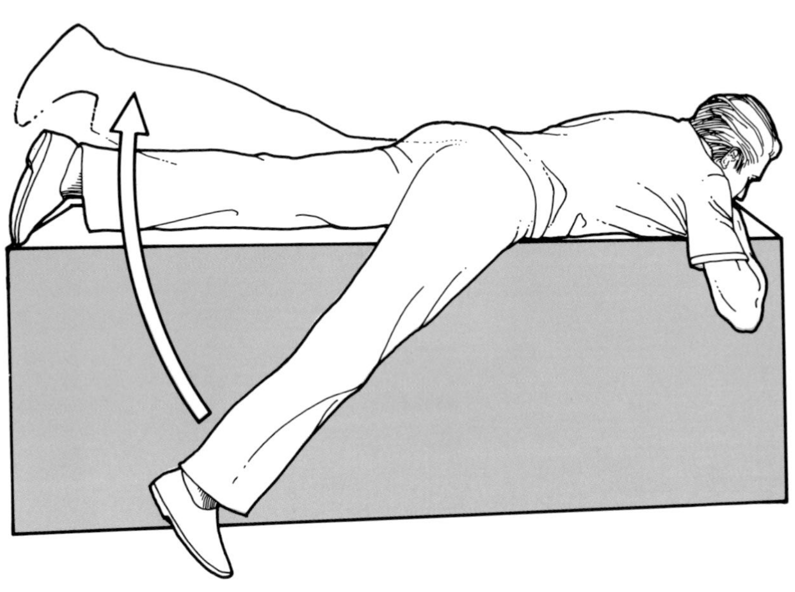

Hip Extension (cont.)

This exercise must be done on an elevated surface, such as an exercise table, a massage table, a bench between rows of lockers, or even a couch at home. This will allow you to lie on your stomach, so that your trunk, pelvis, and left leg are on a flat surface, and your right leg can reach down to the floor. Lift your right leg as high as you can, keeping the knee straight; hold, then return to your original position. Repeat on the opposite side. ■

EXERCISE 30

Wall Squats

This exercise strengthens the quadriceps, which straightens the knee. It helps provide lower body power and stability in the golf swing.

Stand with your back against a wall, legs slightly apart, and feet about 12 inches from the wall. Slide down slowly, keeping your back against the wall, while bending your knees as though you were sitting in a chair. Hold this squat position for a count of 10, and return to the starting position. As you get stronger, try holding this sitting position for up to 20 seconds, so that your muscles feel totally fatigued.

One cautionary note: don't feel you must actually try to reach a chair-sitting position at first, for you may not be able to get back up. ■

Wall Squats (cont.)

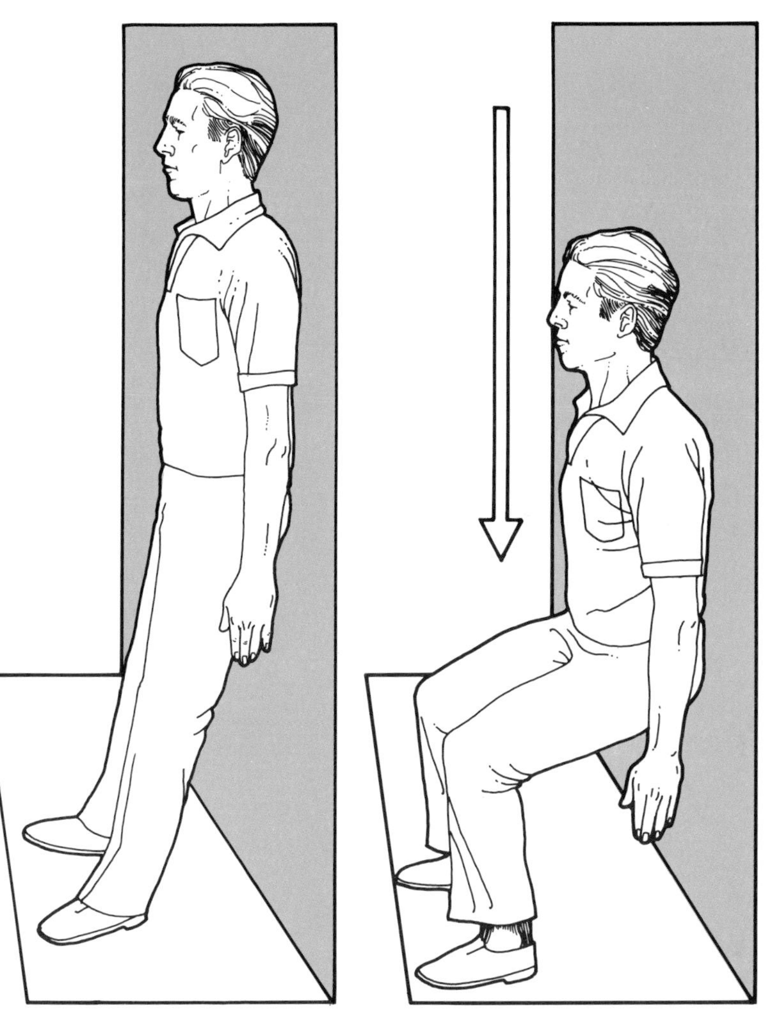

CHAPTER FOUR

Weight Training Equipment

If you have access to weight training equipment, here are some examples of how you can adapt certain strengthening exercises shown in Chapter Three. We have used the DP Gympac™ to illustrate these exercises, courtesy of the Diversified Products' booklet, "Golf Fitness Instruction Course."

Many people have been hesitant to use exercise equipment, they worry that this use could lead to muscular overdevelopment. The important thing to remember when using fitness equipment is that you are working toward an increase in strength and endurance. The goal is *not* to lift to maximum resistance which causes overdevelopment, but to work out lifting less than maximum resistance for many repetitions.

Stretching or a good warmup are very important before exercising with weight training equipment. After you are warmed up, begin with low resistance levels and increase them only after you are able to do several sets of 10-15 repetitions each.

POSITION 1

Chest Muscles

Chest Muscles (cont.)

Starting position: Lower pulley with double handle.

■ Stand sideways to the DP Gympac™, so that the cable does not touch the cover. Grasp both handles in one hand. Keep the arm very slightly bent. Spread the feet wide and bend both knees for balance.

■ Pull the handles across the body in a sweeping arc, palm leading, similar to a forehand racqetball stroke. Exhale as you pull.

■ Return to the starting position while inhaling. Perform 10 to 15 repetitions, 1 to 3 sets. Repeat the exercise with the other arm.

If you have back problems, it is better to sit on a bench and then pull up and across the body.

You may also use the upper pulley attachment with the double handle to pull down hard across the body while sitting. ■

Position 2

Bent-over Row

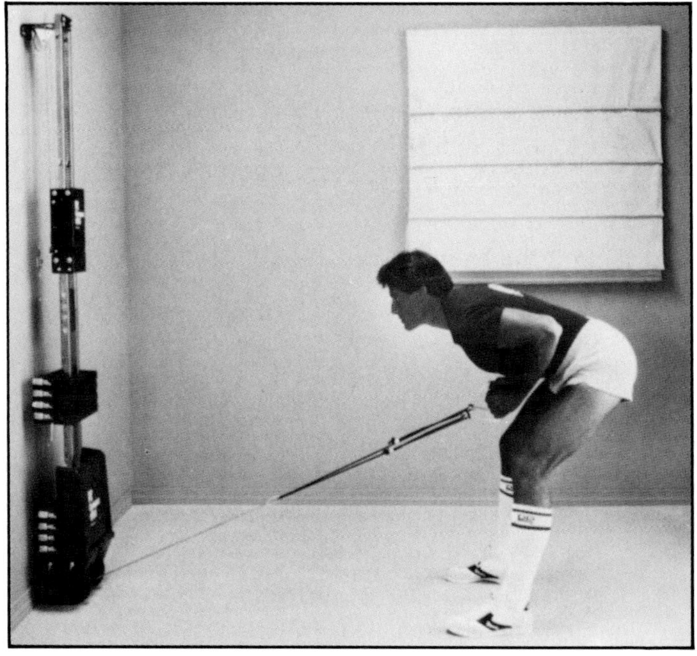

Bent-over Row (cont.)

Starting position: Lower pulley position.

■ Stand facing the DP Gympac™ so that the cable does not touch the cover. Grasp both handles with palms facing each other. Bend forward at the hips with slightly bent knees. Hold the back flat and extend both arms downward and toward the DP Gympac™.

■ Pull the handles upward and inward to the abdomen while exhaling.

■ Return slowly to the starting position while inhaling. Perform 10 to 15 repetitions, 1 to 3 sets.

If you have low back pain, it is better to do this exercise seated with the pulley on the upper hook up. ■

POSITION 3

Internal Rotation Exercise

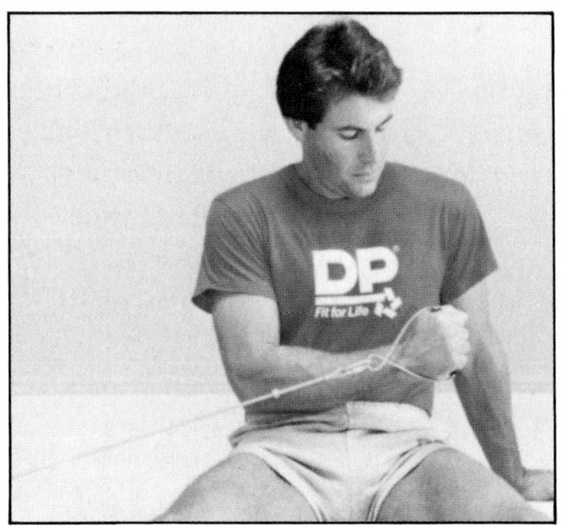

Internal Rotation Exercise (cont.)

Starting position: Lower pulley with one handle.

■ Sit on the floor sideways to the DP Gympac™. Grasp the stirrup handle with your thumb up and your elbow pressed against your side.

■ Slowly pull the handle across in front of you until your forearm is pressed against your abdomen. Exhale as you pull.

■ Return slowly and smoothly to the starting position while inhaling.

Perform 10 repetitions, 3 sets. ■

POSITION 4

Wrist Flexion

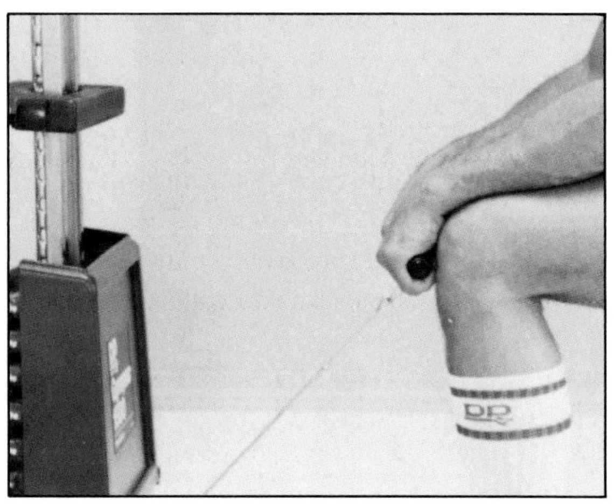

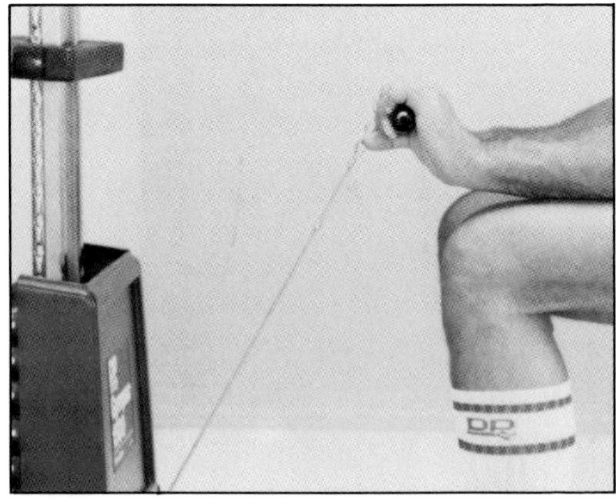

Wrist Flexion (cont.)

Starting position: Lower pulley with short bar.

■ Sit on the end of the bench facing the DP Gympac™ lower pulley. Grasp the short bar with an under grip and palms up. Rest both forearms along the top of your thighs. Bend both wrists downward and allow the bar to slide to your fingertips.

■ Grip firmly and curl both wrists upward as far as possible. Keep both forearms against your thighs. Breathe normally throughout the exercise.

■ Return slowly to the starting position.

Perform 8 to 12 repetitions, 1 to 4 sets. ■

POSITION 5

Wrist Extension

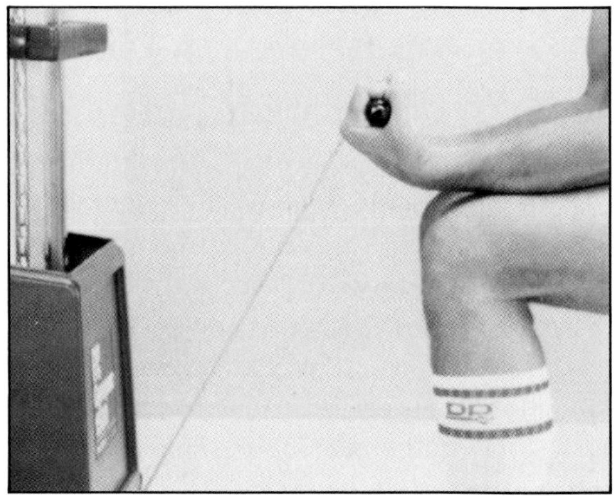

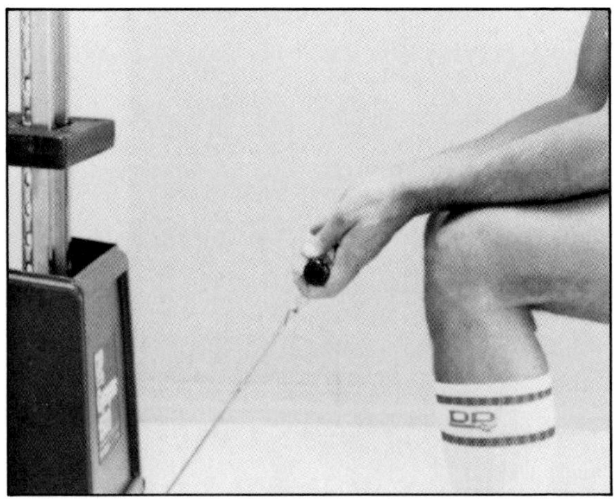

Wrist Extension (cont.)

Starting position: Lower pulley with short bar.

■ Take the same position as in the previous exercise except that you grasp the bar with an overgrip, and palms down.

■ Bend your wrists downward as far as possible.

■ Turn your wrist upward as far as possible. Breathe normally throughout the exercise.

Perform 8 to 12 repetitions, 1 to 4 sets. ■

POSITION 6

Side Leg Lift

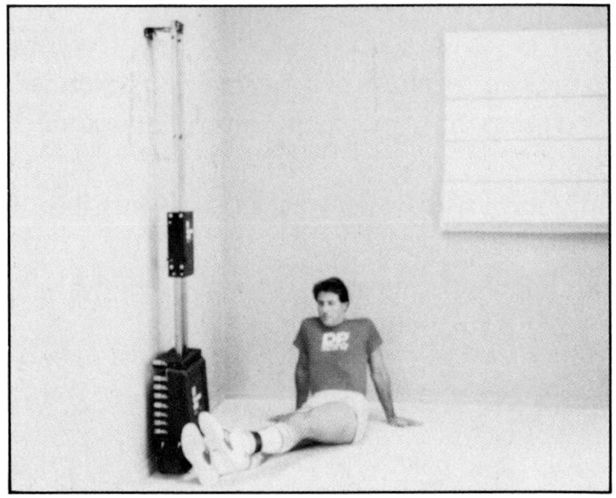

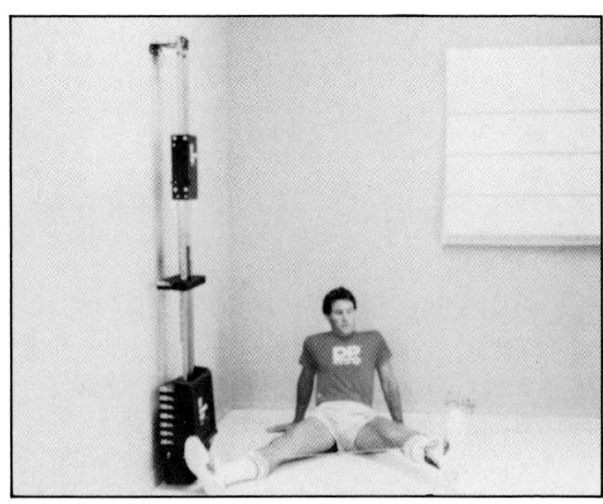

Side Leg Lift (cont.)

Starting position: Lower pulley.

■ Sit sideways to the DP Gympac™ with both feet together, arms to the rear and with both hands on the floor for balance. The ankle strap is attached to the left ankle.

■ Lift the left leg slightly off the floor. Swing the left leg to the left as far as possible, keeping the toes pointed. Exhale as you swing the leg outward.

■ Return the left leg to the starting position while inhaling.

Perform 10 to 20 repetitions, 1 to 4 sets. Repeat the exercise with the right leg. ■

POSITION 7

Leg Lifts

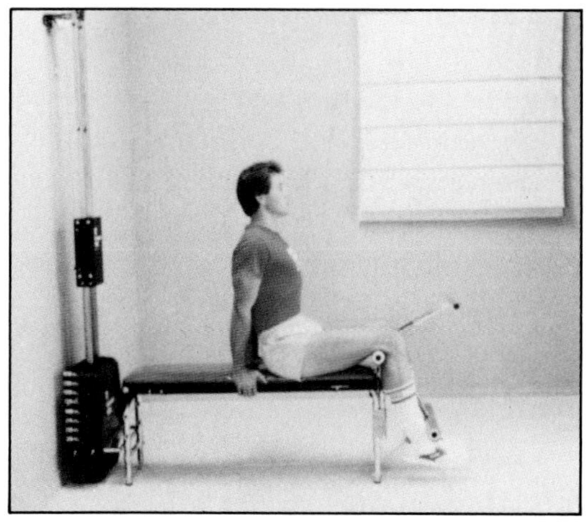

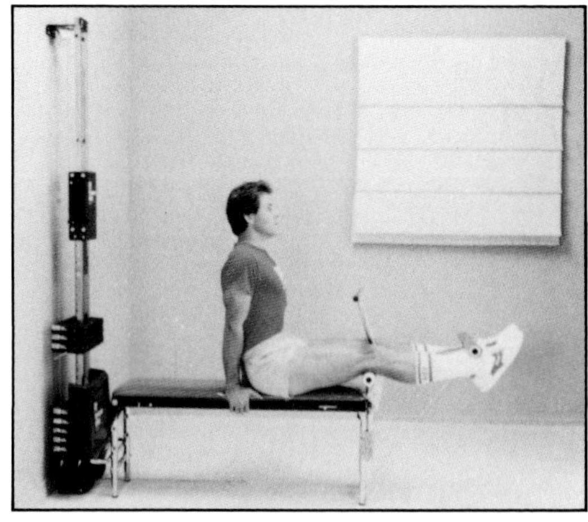

Leg Lifts (cont.)

Starting position: Leg lift/leg curl/row assembly attached to bench.

■ Sit on the bench with both legs positioned over the padded top bar of the leg lift. Ankles are then placed under the center of the lower bar. Place both hands to the rear with arms straight.

■ Lift the bar upward until the legs are straight. Exhale. Hold the up position for two seconds.

■ Lower the legs to the starting position while inhaling.

Perform 10 to 15 repetitions, 1 to 3 sets. ■

INDEX